£7.9-

GREAT CHARACTERS OF THE BIBLE

Clarence E. Macartney

kregel
PUBLICATIONS

Grand Rapids, MI 49501

Great Characters of the Bible by Clarence E. Macartney

Published in 1996 by Kregel Publications, a division of Kregel, Inc., P. O. Box 2607, Grand Rapids, MI 49501. Kregel Publications provides trusted, biblical publications for Christian growth and service. Your comments and suggestions are valued.

Cover Photograph: Copyright © 1996 Kregel, Inc.
Cover and Book Design: Alan G. Hartman

Library of Congress Cataloging-in-Publication Data
Macartney, Clarence Edward Noble, 1879–1957
   [Man who forgot]
   Great characters of the Bible / Clarence E. Macartney.
      p. cm.
   Originally published: The man who forgot. New York: Abingdon Press, 1956.
   1. Bible—Biography—Sermons. 2. Sermons, American. 3. Presbyterian Church—Sermons. I. Title.
BS571.5.M35   1996   220.9'2—dc20   95–32062
                                               CIP

ISBN 0-8254-3282-0

      1 2 3 4 5 Printing / Year 00 99 98 97 96

Printed in the United States of America

CONTENTS

1

THE MAN WHO FORGOT— THE CHIEF BUTLER

Yet did not the chief butler remember Joseph, but forgat him (Gen. 40:23).

The miserable ingrate! When the butler was a criminal in the jail, not knowing what a day would bring to him—liberty or bondage, life or death—he did not forget Joseph.

The chief butler and the chief baker had offended their lord, and Pharaoh had committed them to the dungeon. The captain of the guard gave them into the keeping of the young Hebrew captive, Joseph, who was in prison because of the hatred of a wicked woman whose advances he had scorned. Everybody down in Egypt seems to have had the habit of dreaming, from the king on his throne to the baker who made his bread. Both the chief butler and the chief baker dreamed during that first night in the prison, and their dreams left them filled with sadness and apprehension. Joseph himself was an exile from his home, sold by his brothers into Egypt and now in prison charged with a crime he did not commit. One would think it was he who needed comfort. But he was kindhearted, this Hebrew exile. When he saw the two prisoners looking so sad in the morning, his heart went out to them in sympathy. His own problem made him only the more sympathetic with others in their troubles, instead of hardening and souring him and making him look with suspicion upon all mankind.

One of the best ways to cure your own sorrow is to take an interest in the sorrows of others. Joseph sat where they sat, and therefore he was able to meet them on a common footing and give them what cheer he could. But Joseph, while not boasting that he could tell them what they wished to know, said that with the help of God he would interpret their dreams. "Do not interpretations belong to God? tell me them, I pray you."

First, the chief butler told his dream:

> In my dream, behold, a vine was before me; and in the vine were three branches: and it was as though it budded, and her blossoms shot forth; and the clusters thereof brought forth ripe grapes: and Pharaoh's cup was in my hand: and I took the grapes, and pressed them into Pharaoh's cup, and I gave the cup into Pharaoh's hand. And Joseph said unto him, This is the interpretation of it: The three branches are three days: Yet within three days shall Pharaoh lift up thine head, and restore thee unto thy place: and thou shalt deliver Pharaoh's cup into his hand, after the former manner when thou wast his butler. But think on me when it shall be well with thee, and shew kindness, I pray thee, unto me, and make mention of me unto Pharaoh, and bring me out of this house: for indeed I was stolen away out of the land of the Hebrews: and here also have I done nothing that they should put me into the dungeon.

Then the chief baker related his dream:

> I also was in my dream, and, behold, I had three white baskets on my head: and in the uppermost basket there was of all manner of bakemeats for Pharaoh; and the birds did eat them out of the basket upon my head. And Joseph answered and said, This is the interpretation thereof: The three baskets are three days: Yet within three days shall Pharaoh lift up thy head from off thee, and shall hang thee on a tree; and the birds shall eat thy flesh from off thee.

On the third day the interpretation of the dreams came true. Both of the men were taken out of the jail and brought to the court of Pharaoh. There the chief butler was restored to his office and held again the cup of Pharaoh, but the chief baker was hanged. I fancy I can see Joseph at the dungeon door watching those two men go out. He heard the sad farewell of the baker and the effusive gratitude of the butler, who vowed that the first thing he would do when he was restored to his place would be to put in a word for the Hebrew lad who had interpreted his dream.

Joseph's heart beat high with hope, for now he was sure that he had a friend at court who would state his case to Pharaoh. But the days and the weeks and the months passed by, and still no word came from the chief butler. He cannot completely have forgotten Joseph. For a few weeks at least he must have thought of him the last thing before he went to sleep and the first thing when he arose in the morning. But it was difficult to bring the matter before Pharaoh. Pharaoh might be in a bad humor and commit him again to that dungeon. Then he had fine friends, this butler, and they might wonder at his intimacy with a Hebrew slave. If he did get Joseph out of the dungeon, the youth might be on his hands.

Thus, day by day it became easier for him to postpone that word with Pharaoh in behalf of Joseph, until at length, in the cares and pleasures of his office, Joseph and the promise made to him were completely forgotten. "Yet did not the chief butler remember Joseph, but forgat him." At the end of two years, when Pharaoh had his dreams about the ears of corn and the kine, the butler suddenly remembered Joseph, not out of gratitude, but hoping to win the favor of the king by bringing in a man who could tell him his dream.

Joseph was making rapid progress in the experimental knowledge of the depravity of the human heart. He knew what jealousy could move men to do, for his brothers had sold him into Egypt. He had learned from Potiphar's wife what lust and lying could do. Now he was to discover how one can forget a benefactor. If Joseph had injured this chief butler, the man would not have forgotten him to his dying day; but because Joseph had helped him in the day of trouble, he quickly forgot. "Yet did not the chief butler remember Joseph, but forgat him." O thou most human butler!

Filial Ingratitude

This most popular sin, like all sin, takes many forms and wears many different garments. It appears sometimes in the form of filial ingratitude. "Honor thy father and mother, for this is right in the sight of the Lord." Happy the son who can honor a mother and a father who were all to him that parents ought to be. But even when this has not been the case, children still owe a debt to the sacred relationship of father and mother, no matter how sinned against or how abused that relationship has been. It is hardly necessary to speak of the extreme cases of filial neglect, for this is not respectable with either man or God. When you hear an infant crying and see its mother go to take it up in her arms and rock it and soothe it with songs and mother-talk, does it remind you that someone must have done likewise to you, in season and out of season? When you see anxious, careworn, sleep-robbed mothers, do you realize the hours of anxious watching and waiting, toil and labor, playing and singing, which you yourself once cost your parents?

I went one summer in Edinburgh to visit Alison Cunningham, the aged nurse of Robert Louis Stevenson, to whom he dedicates his book of verse, with the following lines:

> For the long nights you lay awake
> And watched for my unworthy sake:
> For your most comfortable hand
> That led me through the uneven land:
> For all the story-books you read:
> For all the pains you comforted:
> For all you pitied, all you bore,
> In sad and happy days of yore:—
> My second Mother, my first Wife,
>
> From the sick child, now well and old,
> Take, nurse, the little book you hold!

Those are lines that every mother's son might well frame and hang upon the walls of his room and upon the walls of the chamber of memory.

Some think that Shakespeare sounded the depths of mortal sorrow and suffering in that tremendous scene in *King Lear*, where the aged king and father, cast out by his unnatural daughters, wanders on the gloomy heath at night and utters his apostrophe to wind and rain, thunder and lightning. He had learned how "sharper than a serpent's tooth it is to have a thankless child." Ingratitude in all its degrees is an ugly thing, but most loathsome when it shows itself in a child.

> Ingratitude, thou marble-hearted fiend,
> More hideous, when thou show'st thee in a child,
> Than the sea-monster!

It is always pleasant to look on the other side of this relationship between parents and children and to behold the beauty of gratitude. Thaddeus Stevens, one of America's most powerful and influential statesmen before, during, and after the Civil War, had a devout mother who toiled for her lame son so that he might secure an education. When he had achieved success as a lawyer, he told how it was his delight to give every week a gold piece to his mother so that she might put it in the collection box of the Baptist church which she attended. Every spring and summer, in a cemetery in Lancaster you will find roses and other pleasant flowers beginning to bloom, for in his will Thaddeus Stevens provided that such flowers be planted to keep his mother's grave ever bright and fresh.

In a churchyard at Hamilton, Scotland, is the stone erected by David Livingstone and his brothers and sisters to their godly parents. It bears this inscription:

> To show the resting place of
> Neil Livingstone
> And Agnes Hunter, his wife,
> And to express the thankfulness to God
> Of their children
> For poor and pious parents.

INGRATITUDE TO FRIENDS AND BENEFACTORS

On one occasion Talleyrand, being told that a certain public officer was saying evil things against him, exclaimed: "That surprises me; I have never done him a favor!" When the ministry

of Robert Walpole fell and a hostile vote was being taken in
the House of Commons, Walpole, watching those who voted
against him, said to the one who sat near him: "Young man, I
will tell you the history of all these men as they come in. That
fellow I saved from the gallows. And that one, from starvation.
This other one's son I promoted."

When Jesus healed the ten lepers and sent them off to the
priest to declare themselves and get a certificate of health, only
one returned to give thanks. Jesus was amazed. "Were there
not ten cleansed?" He exclaimed, "Where are the nine?" How
tenacious are our memories of occasional injuries or slights we
receive, but how careless as to benefits!

> Blow, blow, thou winter wind,
>   Thou art not so unkind
> As man's ingratitude;
>   Thy tooth is not so keen,
> Because thou art not seen,
>   Although thy breath be rude.
>
> Freeze, freeze, thou bitter sky,
>   That dost not bite so nigh
> As benefits forgot:
>   Though thou the waters warp,
> Thy sting is not so sharp
>   As friend remember'd not.[1]

In *Gulliver's Travels* Jonathan Swift gives us his opinion of
ingratitude to friends and benefactors when he thus describes
the laws of the Lilliputians:

> Ingratitude is among them a capital crime, . . . for they reason thus,
> that whoever makes ill returns to his benefactor, must needs be a com-
> mon enemy to the rest of mankind, from whom he hath received no
> obligation, and therefore such a man is not fit to live.

In the laws of the Spartans, however, it was different. When

---

1. Shakespeare, *As You Like It*, 2.7.

Lycurgus was asked why his laws provided no penalty for ingratitude, he said, "I have left the punishment of that crime to the gods."

David knew the bitterness of ingratitude. Some friend or counselor had returned evil for good, treachery for confidence; to this David refers in the fifty-fifth psalm. He says he could have stood it if it had been the work of one who hated him, or some open enemy, or a stranger; what hurt him deeply was that it was by a former friend.

> For it was not an enemy that reproached me; then I could have borne it: neither was it he that hated me that did magnify himself against me; then I would have hid myself from him: But it was thou, a man mine equal, my guide, and mine acquaintance. We took sweet counsel together, and walked unto the house of God in company.

The wounds that hurt most are not those inflicted by the enemy or the stranger, but those which we have received in the house of our friend. "I was wounded in the house of my friends." It was not the dagger of Brutus but the changed heart of Brutus that slew Caesar.

> For when the noble Caesar saw him stab,
> Ingratitude, more strong than traitors' arms,
> Quite vanquish'd him: then burst his mighty heart;
> And, in his mantle muffling up his face,
> Even at the base of Pompey's statue,
> Which all the while ran blood, great Caesar fell.[2]

On the other side, beautiful are the instances of gratitude on the part of those who did not forget their benefactors. General Grant arrived in New York in 1854 after he had resigned, under a cloud, from the army in California; he was without funds and still far from his Ohio home. In this difficulty he went to call on a West Point friend and comrade in the Mexican War, Simon Bolivar Buckner. Buckner generously supplied him with funds so that he could reach his home

---

2. Shakespeare, *Julius Caesar*, 3.2.

in Ohio. Eight years afterward when Grant captured Fort
Donelson in February 1862, the surrender was made by General Buckner, the other officers having fled. In a speech delivered long after at a Grant birthday dinner, Buckner told what
had happened there at Fort Donelson:

> Under these circumstances I surrendered to General Grant. I had at a
> previous time befriended him, and it has been justly said that he never
> forgot an act of kindness. I met him on the boat [Grant's headquarters
> boat], and he followed me when I went to my quarters. He left the officers
> of his own army and followed me, with that modest manner peculiar to
> him, into the shadow, and there he tendered me his purse. It seems to me
> that in the modesty of his nature he was afraid the light would witness that
> act of generosity, and sought to hide it from the world.

One of the charming things about the letters of Paul is the
way in which he makes mention of the different friends who
have done him a kindness: "Greet Priscilla and Aquila my
helpers in Christ Jesus: who for my life laid down their own
necks." "Greet Amplias my beloved in the Lord." "Salute Rufus
chosen in the Lord, and his mother and mine." "The Lord
give mercy unto the house of Onesiphorus; for he oft refreshed
me, and was not ashamed of my chains." And so down the long
list of those who had shown him any kindness. The last message for Onesiphorus was given when Paul was "ready to be
offered up" and his own death was at hand. Yet in that hour
the memory of a friend refreshed him.

Like a sudden glow of sunlight appearing through the black
clouds at the close of a stormy winter's day is that last act in
the tragedy of King Saul. When Saul had fallen on Gilboa's
mount, the Philistines cut off his head and stripped the armor
from the body, sending the armor to different parts of the
Philistine country as monuments to the victory over their great
foe. His body they nailed to the wall of Beth-shan. The news
soon spread throughout Israel of the defeat and the death of
Saul and his sons. At length the tidings came to Jabesh-gilead,
away across the Jordan, the town that Saul had saved out of
the hand of the Ammonites when first he became king. No
other city in all Israel raised a finger to save the body of Saul

from desecration. But these men of Jabesh-gilead remembered the kindness he had done them years before. In gratitude for that deed, these men, taking their lives in their hands, "went all night" to the Philistine stronghold. Removing the body of Saul and the bodies of his sons from the wall of Beth-shan, they brought them to Jabesh and burned them there, burying the ashes under the tamarisk tree. This was followed by seven days of fasting.

Can you think now of anyone who has helped you, strengthened you, guided you, supported you when you were weak, warned you when tempted, lifted you up when you were falling? Then crown yourself with the beauty of gratitude. Write the letter, send the greeting, say the word that can cheer a soul around whom winter's gloom may be gathering. Like the Jabeshites, you can honor the relics of the dead; still better, you can cheer the living.

INGRATITUDE TO GOD

All ingratitude is a sin against God. In his terrible, but true, arraignment of fallen human nature, Paul, in the first chapter of the letter to the Romans, describes man's sin and corruption in the terms of ingratitude:

> When they knew God, they glorified him not as God, neither were thankful; but became vain in their imaginations, and their foolish heart was darkened. . . . [They] changed the truth of God into a lie, and worshiped and served the creature more than the Creator.

For the common blessings of our lives how little thought we take and how little thanks we give! As certain birds do not reveal the brilliance of their plumage until they spread their wings in flight, so many of our blessings are not appreciated until they have departed. "Have you given any thanks to God today for your reason?" said one man to another as he stopped him on the street. Somewhat startled by the solemn look of the man, the other answered, "I confess that I have not." "Go then, and do so instantly," replied the man, "for I have lost mine!"

A popular lecturer of the last quarter of the nineteenth century had a lecture on "Sunshine" that he gave all over the country. Having arrived at a city where he was to give his lecture, he was passing through the station with a member of the lecture committee who had met him when he saw a stretcher being carried by on which lay a paralyzed man. Pausing, he looked at the man on the stretcher and said to the young man who had met him: "Whenever I see anything like that, I say to myself, 'Every misery missed is a new blessing.'"

When that celebrated mariner and philosopher Robinson Crusoe was wrecked on his lonely isle, he drew up two columns that he called "the evil and the good," and set over against the evil, the good. He was cast on a desolate island, but he was alive and not drowned, as were all his ship's company. He was divided from mankind and banished from human society, but he was not starving. He had no clothes, but the climate was so hot he did not need them. He was without means of defense, but he saw no wild beasts such as he had seen on the coast of Africa. He had not a soul to speak to, but God had sent the ship so near the shore that he could get from it all things necessary for his wants. Hence, he concluded that there was no condition in the world so miserable but there was something negative or something positive in it to be thankful for.

Paul was the man who said, "In every thing give thanks," and was himself able to do so. Even on that storm-driven vessel, tossing in the night off the shore of Malta, with the waves breaking in thunderous roars against the granite cliffs a few ship-lengths off, Paul persuaded the ship's company to take some food. But first of all, before partaking of it himself, he gave thanks to God.

David is spoken of in the Bible as a man "after God's own heart." One reason, no doubt, is that David, although he sinned so deeply, confessed his sin, repented, and sought after God. But another reason was his unfailing thankfulness, even in the midst of his sorrows and adversities. In David's hour of triumph, when after all his trials he became king, he did not celebrate his victory by taking vengeance upon his enemies. Instead, he wondered if there were any left of the house of Saul, that he might show the "kindness of God" to him.

He was thinking, of course, of Saul's son Jonathan—Jonathan whose love to him was "wonderful, passing the love of women"—who had protected him against the murderous vengeance of Saul. When the king learned that there was a lame son of Jonathan still alive, Mephibosheth, David sent for him and established him in the palace, saying to him, "Fear not: for I will surely shew thee kindness for Jonathan thy father's sake." David thus remembered the kindness of Jonathan; especially did he recall that night in the wood of Ziph when, with his fortunes at their lowest ebb and his faith in God shaken, Jonathan came to him and "strengthened his hand in God."

Show, then, your gratitude to God in deeds of kindness and goodness to others, as David did to the son of Jonathan, and by your belief and trust in God—that God from whom all blessings flow. Forget not all His benefits! Paul had a vast vocabulary, but when he came to speak of the kindness of God to man in Christ his vocabulary failed him. All he could say was, "Thanks be unto God for his unspeakable gift!" The only thing you can give to God is your thanks.

2

GOD IN HISTORY—CYRUS

I girded thee, though thou hast not known me (Isa. 45:5).

Cyrus, king of the Persians and conqueror of Sardis and Babylon, was one of the nobler pagans of antiquity. As in the case of so many of the characters who achieved world empire and fame, legend and fancy have busied themselves with the origins of his life and history. One story makes him an outcast on the mountains who was suckled by a dog and educated by a shepherd; another tale makes his nurse and deliverer a shepherd's wife. But when he emerged upon the stage of great events and became a conqueror whose empire stretched from India to Asia Minor, we can follow his history with a degree of certainty. All the sketches of his life show him as a man and ruler with singular loftiness of spirit and kindness. When he captured Sardis, the capital of Lydia, Croesus the king was condemned to be burned, as was the cruel custom of the age. As Croesus was about to be consigned to the flames, Cyrus chanced to overhear him repeat a saying he had heard once on the lips of the Spartan philosopher Solon, "Count no man happy until the end." Struck with this sentiment, Cyrus ordered the king set at liberty.

As a child Cyrus was taught to shun the intoxicating cup. Once, on a visit to his royal grandfather in Media, Cyrus asked to be permitted to act as the cupbearer at the feast. He did everything to perfection and was warmly applauded by the nobles present, who were delighted with his mimicry of the cupbearer, stepping grandly and solemnly about. The king, too, praised him but called his attention to one omission—he had neglected to taste the wine, as the cupbearer always did, before handing it to the king. Cyrus said he had not tasted the wine because he thought it had been poisoned. Asked why he thought that, he answered: "It was poisoned the other day when you made a feast for your friends on your birthday. I know by the effects. The things you do not allow us boys to do, you did yourself; for you were rude and very noisy. You could not even stand erect and steady. So I thought that the wine which produced these effects must have been poisoned."

According to the account of the historian Herodotus,[1] Cyrus captured Babylon by diverting the waters of the Euphrates into an artificial lake and marching his soldiers into the city by way of the dry riverbed, the gates of the city having been left open on a night when the court and the nobles were having a drunken revel.

One of the first acts of Cyrus after he overthrew Babylon was to issue a proclamation permitting the Jews, who had been for seventy years captives in Babylon, to return to Jerusalem and rebuild their temple. He also restored to them the sacred vessels which had been carried down to Babylon when Nebuchadnezzar captured Jerusalem. We have the record of this gracious deed on the part of Cyrus, a turning point in the history of the Jews, in the first chapter of the book of Ezra. It was in every way a remarkable proclamation:

> Thus saith Cyrus king of Persia, The Lord God of heaven hath given me all the kingdoms of the earth; and he hath charged me to build him an house at Jerusalem, which is in Judah. Who is there among you of all his people? his God be with him, and let him go up to Jerusalem, which is in Judah, and build the house of the Lord God of Israel, (he is the God,) which is in Jerusalem. And whosoever remaineth in any place where he sojourneth, let the men of his place help him with silver, and with gold, and with goods, and with beasts, beside the freewill offering for the house of God that is in Jerusalem.

---

1. Herodotus *History* 1.190.

If this proclamation by Cyrus, so contrary to the custom of the age and of conquerors, is remarkable, even more remarkable is the prediction of it by the prophet Isaiah:

> That saith to Jerusalem, Thou shalt be inhabited; and to the cities of Judah, Ye shall be built, and I will raise up the decayed places thereof: That saith to the deep, Be dry, and I will dry up thy rivers: That saith of Cyrus, He is my shepherd, and shall perform all my pleasure: even saying to Jerusalem, Thou shalt be built; and to the temple, Thy foundation shall be laid.
>
> Thus saith the Lord to his anointed, to Cyrus, whose right hand I have holden, to subdue nations before him; and I will loose the loins of kings, to open before him the two leaved gates; and the gates shall not be shut; I will go before thee, and make the crooked places straight: I will break in pieces the gates of brass, and cut in sunder the bars of iron: And I will give thee the treasures of darkness, and hidden riches of secret places, that thou mayest know that I, the Lord, which call thee by thy name, am the God of Israel. For Jacob my servant's sake, and Israel mine elect, I have even called thee by thy name: I have surnamed thee, though thou hast not known me. I am the Lord, and there is none else, there is no God beside me: I girded thee, though thou hast not known me: That they may know from the rising of the sun, and from the west, that there is none beside me. I am the Lord, and there is none else (Isa. 44:26–45:6.)

Thus we see that more than a century before he appeared on the stage of history, Cyrus is called by his name, his great conquests are sketched, and his part in the restoration of the Jews and the rebuilding of the temple is predicted. He is named as God's "shepherd," who shall do God's will. It has been surmised by some that Daniel, who was alive when Babylon fell, may have called the attention of Cyrus to the prediction of Isaiah, and perhaps also to Jeremiah's prediction as to the length of the captivity.[2] But whether it was by the suggestion of the prophet Daniel, or by a special revelation and inspiration of the Holy Spirit, the great pagan king fulfilled the purpose of God. Cyrus did not know him as God, yet God said of

---

2. Jer. 25:11–12; 29:10; see also Dan. 9:2.

him: "I have even called thee by thy name. . . . I girded thee, though thou hast not known me."

GOD IN HISTORY

Very significant and very impressive is what God said of Cyrus: "I girded thee, though thou hast not known me." There we have the majestic doctrine of God in history. This truth never received a grander setting forth than in Paul's address to the philosophers on Mars' hill: "[God] hath made of one blood all nations of men for to dwell on all the face of the earth, and hath determined the times before appointed, and the bounds of their habitation." This means that history is not a happen-so, not an accident. It means that the supreme actor on the stage of history is God; the great epochs, the great nations, and the great personalities are but the brief embodiment and the transient realization of His eternal purpose.

But what of the darker side of history? The doctrine of divine providence occasions no trouble when we are dealing with nobler heathen like Cyrus or men like Daniel, Isaiah, Paul, Augustine, Luther, or Lincoln. But what about the tyrants and oppressors, the monsters of iniquity? What about the evildoers of our own day? What about the two terrible wars, which in a single generation turned the sun into darkness and the moon into blood?

God must be in these terrible chapters of the world's history; otherwise, one would have to exclude God from a great part of history. In his powerful description of the battle and the battlefield of Sedan, where the German army conquered the French in 1870, Victor Hugo says: "In the midst of the terrible plain I saw thee, O Thou Invisible One." The Invisible One is always present. The history of the world is the judgment of the world; as a great history-maker, Cromwell, put it: "What are all our histories, but God throwing down and trampling under foot whatsoever He hath not planted?"

That God can use the most terrible chapters, the most wicked acts, and the most wicked people for His great and beneficent purposes is witnessed to by the history of Christianity. Upon what does Christianity stand? With all its hopes and with all

its joys and all its inspiration, it stands upon the most wicked
and terrible deed that the earth ever saw or upon which the
sun ever looked down—the nailing of the Son of God to the
cross. We need not pause in anxiety and trouble over the dread-
ful deeds and the wicked people of our day and generation,
when we can remember how God has made the wrath of man
to praise Him in the death of Christ on the Cross.

At the outbreak of World War II, in view of the danger to
which the Netherlands was subjected, the Dutch prime minister spoke these words to his nation and its colonies:

> What the future will bring us remains in the hands of God. It is
> possible that hardships await us which we cannot foresee at this moment;
> but even then this must never bring us to a mood of despair. If we do our
> duty, we can await the result calmly and leave it to Him who knows what
> we need, and who never made a mistake yet. However high the waves
> may go, we know that our Father holds the wheel, and we will keep a
> spirit of calmness and cheerfulness. We end with a song on our lips, and
> more so in our hearts, "Order us in Thy ways."

After that Christian statesman spoke those words, Holland
had its deluge of violence, terror, blood, destruction, and death.
But in that terrible disaster there were hundreds of thousands
in Holland who took refuge in the divine appointment of God
and still prayed, "Order us in Thy Ways."

PROVIDENCE IN OUR LIVES

There can be no providence in history without providence in the lives of individuals, and there can be no general providence without a particular providence. God girds
people even when they do not know Him or when they
resist Him. In our own personal lives, even when we knew it
not and knew Him not, in His providential care God has
used us and girded us.

The objections that are raised against the doctrine of providence lose their weight when we write God with a capital *G*. It
has been said that it is unthinkable that God should have a
hand in or order the multitude of details that go into the

history of a single life, not to mention millions of lives through countless ages. That would indeed be an insurmountable difficulty for a finite mind, but not for the infinite mind of God, without whom, Christ said, not even a sparrow—poorest and meanest of the birds—falls frozen or starved to the ground.

Another objection is that it would be unworthy of God to deal with so many small events. Aristotle said that it would derogate from the dignity of God if He were to take part in the small events of a man's life, just as it would be beneath the dignity of a Xerxes to perform menial and ordinary tasks. But what is a small event? And what is a great event? What could be more apparent than that the seemingly trivial and insignificant events have been hinges upon which have swung the mighty doors of history and of destiny?

Take it in your own life. Little events have made you and brought you where you are. You came to a city expecting to spend the night, and there you have spent the rest of your life. You turned down one street instead of another, not knowing why, but life would have been altogether different for you if you had chosen the other street. You wrote, or did not write, a letter, and history proceeded out of that act or that omission. You went into a room and saw a face; it was the face of your wife, your posterity. Thus, little events, apparently chance happenings, are links in the chain of destiny.

God's providence is universal. It takes in all events, "all his creatures and all their actions," as the Catechism puts it. On the wall of the chapel at the first church where I was pastor there was a memorial tablet to a devout Sunday school teacher who had a sudden and, what seemed to her friends, untimely end. The inscription spoke of how she was suddenly removed by "a sorrowful Providence." I have often pondered over that phrase "a sorrowful Providence." It was indeed a sad occasion for her friends and her family; yet they had faith to understand that there was a providence in her taking off.

Sometimes you hear people telling how, by a kind providence, their lives were spared in some accident. They were saved from injury and death either because they did not take the train, or the plane, or the ship that met with disaster, or because in some unaccountable way the shaft of death missed them. But what about those who did take the ship, or the train, or the plane and were killed? Shall we exclude providence from their deaths? John Bunyan was drafted as a soldier in the Civil War in England to take part in the siege of Leicester. As he was just about ready to go forward with his company, another requested to go in his place. "He took my place, and coming to the siege, as he stood sentinel he was shot in the head with a musket bullet and died." That providence saved John Bunyan for his mighty labors for the kingdom of God. But there was a providence also in the death of the soldier who took his place.

God's providence operates not only in the striking and spectacular events of life but in the general flow of events. John Witherspoon, president of Princeton and signer of the Declaration of Independence, lived at Rocky Hill, some distance from the town. One day a neighbor came rushing into his study and asked him to give thanks together with him because, driving from Rocky Hill, his horse had run away, the buggy was smashed, but he escaped death. Witherspoon responded: "I can tell you a far more remarkable providence than that. I have driven over that road hundreds of times. My horse never ran away, my buggy never was smashed, I was never hurt."

In heaven there was once a debate as to who was the greatest monument of God's grace. All breasts were bared and all secrets were told as the redeemed sought to pay tribute to the grace of God. One after another related the sin or transgression out of which Christ had delivered him. At length the choice was settling down upon one man who seemed to have committed all sins. Iniquity after iniquity he related as he turned the ghastly pages of his autobiography. And then he told how on his deathbed Christ came and saved him as He had saved the thief on the cross. But just before the vote was taken, another of the redeemed stepped forward and asked to tell his story. It was this. He had come to know and love Christ as a child and had followed Him all the days of his life, and by God's grace he had been kept from the sins and transgressions which the others had committed. Then the vote was taken. It was not the drunkard, the thief, the adulterer, the perjurer, the murderer, nor the blasphemer, who was selected as the greatest monument to the grace of God but this man who had followed Christ all his days and had been kept from gross sin.

Providence works with a high purpose, and that purpose is the development and the purification of our souls. When the ten-year-old son of President-elect Pierce was killed before the eyes of his shocked parents in a railway accident in 1852, the bereaved mother would not permit her husband to join with others in a suit against the railroad for damages because she regarded her child's death as a special providence for the President-elect, that he might be the better fitted for the responsibilities of his high office.

Trust in Providence delivers us from fear. All of us go out in the morning not knowing what is in store for us or what will happen to us before the evening comes. But we know this, that we cannot drift beyond His love and care. Faith can always discern God's purpose in the events of life. That pillar of cloud that led and protected the children of Israel as they came out of Egypt was light and guidance to the Hebrews; on the side toward their pursuers it was darkness. To the eye of faith God's acts are beneficent and wise. It is not necessary just at the time for us to know and to see how that is so. But we can wait upon God and He will bring it to pass. Joseph must have pondered the purpose of God in his life when he was put in the pit by his brothers, sold as a slave into Egypt, and then cast into the dungeon on a false accusation. But one day he learned that purpose and said to his brothers, "Ye thought evil against me; but God meant it unto good." Ponder over that verse in the Apocalypse, "There was silence in heaven about the space of half an hour." Then all questions shall be answered and all problems solved in the eternal light that shines upon the lives of the redeemed.

At thirty-two years of age William Cowper passed through the great crisis of his life. In four different ways—by poison, by drowning, by the knife, and by hanging—he tried to end his life. Then one morning, in a moment of strange cheerfulness, he opened his Bible and read a verse in the letter to the Romans and almost immediately received strength to believe and rejoice in the forgiving power of God. Not immediately afterward, but some years later, when he had passed through a rich Christian experience and had written many beautiful hymns, he sat down one day and summed up his faith in God's dealings with him and with other men in his great hymn on Divine Providence:

> God moves in a mysterious way
>   His wonders to perform;
> He plants His footsteps in the sea,
>   And rides upon the storm.
>
> Deep in unfathomable mines
>   Of never-failing skill,
> He treasures up His bright designs,
>   And works His sovereign will.
>
> Ye fearful saints, fresh courage take;
>   The clouds ye so much dread
> Are big with mercy, and shall break
>   In blessings on your head.
>
> Blind unbelief is sure to err,
>   And scan His work in vain:
> God is His own Interpreter,
>   And He will make it plain.

3

MORTAL ERROR, IMMORTAL TRUTH—HEROD THE GREAT

When Herod was dead (Matt. 2:19).

W hen Herod was dead!" Literally, "When Herod was *ended*." That is the only good thing about bad men—finally, they die; they are ended.

The Bible is a book of powerful contrasts. Its characters stand up against one another in overwhelming comparison: Cain and Abel, Jacob and Esau, Pharaoh and Moses, Elijah and Jezebel, John the Baptist and Herod Antipas, Judas and John, Paul and Nero; and here, the two kings of the Jews—Herod the Great and Jesus.

Whatever else Herod was great at, he was certainly great at murder. Few have surpassed him in that art. He murdered three of his sons, Alexander, Aristobulus and Antipater, giving the order for the murder of the third son when he himself lay groaning on his deathbed. He drowned Aristobulus, the high priest, and brother of his queen. He strangled that queen, the beautiful Mariamne, the crime for which he suffered such tortures of remorse. These are only a few of the crimes and bloody deeds of this wicked man who was king of the Jews when Jesus was born.

Smitten with incurable suspicion and jealousy, Herod at length developed an incurable disease. When death was drawing nigh, Herod, lying in misery in his ivory palace at Jericho, realized that the people would rejoice when they heard the king was dead. He gave orders, therefore, for the representatives of the chief families of the land to be shut up in the Hippodrome. And the moment the breath left his body, they were to be put to death so that there might be mourning in the land when he expired.

Such a person was Herod the Great, he who had heard with anxiety the message of the wise men from the East, that they had come to worship the newborn king of the Jews. Their inquiry made Herod a student of the Old Testament and he inquired of his own wise men where Christ was to be born. When he learned that He was to be born in Bethlehem, as the prophet Micah had foretold, he directed the wise men to go there, instructing them when they had found the child to bring him word again so that he too might go and worship the newborn king. But the wise men, after they had found the child and his mother and had presented their gifts of gold, frankincense and myrrh, being warned of God in a dream not to return to Herod, departed for their own country by another way.

When Herod saw that he was mocked by the wise men, his criminal and cruel mind devised the plan which, under ordinary circumstances, would have accomplished the destruction of the newborn king. He gave orders that all children, in Bethlehem and in the country around it, two years old and under should be put to the sword. This slaughter of the innocents filled the land with mourning. On the road from Jerusalem to Bethlehem one passes the towerlike tomb of Rachel, the wife of Jacob, who died there when she gave birth to her second child, Benjamin. Her tomb was there in the days of Jeremiah the prophet. To the frantic fathers and mothers whose children Herod had slaughtered, it seemed as if Rachel, the ancestor of their race, was weeping with them over the woes of her people. Jeremiah had written: "In Rama was there a voice heard, lamentation, and weeping, and great mourning, Rachel weeping for her children, and would not be comforted, because they are not." That verse is one of the Bible's mountain peaks of pathos and sorrow.

But the one child whom Herod wanted to take in this far-flung net of massacre and slaughter escaped its bloody meshes. Being warned by God in a dream, Joseph took the young child and His mother and fled into Egypt. There He was as safe from the persecuting hand of Herod as was Moses, ages before, from the persecuting hand of Pharaoh. But "when Herod was dead," the angel of the Lord appeared to Joseph in Egypt and said, "Arise, and take the young child and his mother, and go into the land of Israel: for they are dead which sought the young child's life."

When Herod was dead! That brief history related above is a summary of the age-long struggle between good and evil, between light and darkness, between the kingdom of God and the kingdom of Satan. When Herod was dead! Always some Herod arises against God and His purpose, but always that Herod dies and the plan of God goes on. When Herod was dead! That is a verse and inscription which can be written at the end of many a dark and cruel chapter in human history. Herod is dead! "They that sought the young child's life are dead!" But the truth lives on.

THE ENEMIES OF CHRIST

Every age produces its Herods and its foes of Christ and His church. At the very beginning of human history God said to the tempter, "I will put enmity between thee and the woman, and between thy seed and her seed; it shall bruise thy head, and thou shalt bruise his heel." Everywhere and in every age that enmity has been made manifest. From the very beginning, evil has made war on the good. Wherever Christ appears—wherever a Christlike person is raised up, or a Christlike institution, or a Christlike purpose—there some sinister, troubled, cruel Herod waits to destroy; for to all that is evil in mankind Christ comes to bring not peace, but a sword. Always, as Milton put it in his great ode, the workers of iniquity feel with Herod "the dreaded infant's hand."

In the Apocalypse of John we have a grand prediction and prefiguration of this age-long conflict. The woman clothed with the sun, wearing a crown of twelve stars on her head, is about to give birth to a child. Before the woman stands the dragon, waiting to devour her child as soon as it is born. But the woman flees into the wilderness, where she has a place prepared by God. The very powers of nature help the woman in her escape from the dragon. The wings of a great eagle carry her into the wilderness, and the earth swallows up the flood which the dragon casts out of his mouth. A strange picture, you say. Yet it is the natural history of good and evil. It is a conflict and a scene which appears and reappears in the age-long drama of human history. Always the dragon waits; yet the child is miraculously preserved.

Sometimes the assault on truth and righteousness takes the form of an attack on the persons of those who represent it on earth. Then it is that wherever and whenever someone has died for Christ and the truth, the blood of the righteous Abel mingles with the blood of the prophets. Pharaoh was the Herod of his day and generation and sought to thwart the purpose of God. He, too, gave his infamous order for the slaughter of the innocents, decreeing that every male child should be cast into the Nile. But maternal love and the compassion of a princess saved Moses that he might carry out the will of God.

In the days of Ahab, the wicked heathen queen, Jezebel, sought to destroy Elijah and all the true prophets of God. In the days of Isaiah and Hezekiah, Sennacherib, the king of Assyria, came up to destroy Jerusalem. In the days of Esther and Mordecai, Haman, the wicked satrap of Ahasuerus, got that monarch's consent for the slaughter of the Jews everywhere. The scribes and the chief priests and the Pharisees accomplished the crucifixion of Jesus, apparently succeeding where Herod had failed, for on His cross was the superscription: The King of the Jews.

When the Gospel was first preached, fierce persecution was the outcome. Saul went everywhere, "breathing out threatenings and slaughter," and he held the garments of those who stoned Stephen. The disciples were scattered abroad. Herod's grandson, who inherited his ability as a murderer, put James, the brother of John, to the sword. Then came the imperial persecution, when a whole empire devoted its energies to stamping out and destroying the church of Christ. Centuries later came the armies of the false prophets, their swords flashing every-where over Europe, as far as Hungary in the east, and to the borders of France in the west.

Sometimes the attack on the truth has taken the form of unbelief, false worship, the perversion of the true doctrine. *Diabolus* stands before the walls of a person's soul and with his smooth speech endeavors to persuade the inhabitants to open the gates of the city to him. It is the age-long temptation to compromise with evil, to unite with the world, to admit false principle. Herod pretended to the wise men that he also would like to go down to Bethlehem and worship the newborn king. False worship has always assailed the cause of Christ in the world. Indeed, so frequent have been the corruptions, so numerous the perversions of the truth, so many the disguises that Satan has worn, so subtle the heresies—from those revealed by Paul in the New Testament, down to the latest religious fraud—so widespread have these been, that one marvels as to how a true church founded on the Bible and the Gospel has always survived.

Very often an unknown Christ has been set up for worship; that is, a Christ unknown to history and to the Scriptures. Sometimes it is a Christ without the Incarnation, sometimes a Christ without the Atonement, sometimes a Christ without the miracles, sometimes a Christ without the Resurrection, sometimes a Christ without the Future Advent, who is set up for the worship of men and women. But always it is "another Christ," not the Christ of the Gospel and the Christ of the ages. Thus the long battle goes on from age to age, and out of the depths Satan draws forth new devices and new and subtle attacks upon Christ and His kingdom.

HEROD ALWAYS DIES

Herod dies, but Christ never dies. "They that sought the young child's life are dead." Every battle against Him comes to a conclusion with that announcement of the angel, "They that sought the young child's life are dead."

Pharaoh thought he could thwart the plan of God and destroy Israel by having the midwives kill all the male children at birth. "But the midwives feared God, and did not as the king of Egypt commanded them, but saved the men children alive." Pharaoh then ordered that every male child should be cast into the river Nile. But the parents of Moses, the one destined to become the deliverer of Israel, hid him among the flags in an ark of bulrushes. Thus it was that the very river which had been chosen by the monster, Pharaoh, for the death of Moses, became, in the providence of God, the agent of the child's salvation.

Jezebel gave orders for the destruction of the prophets of Jehovah, Elijah in particular, but God spared the life of Elijah and left Himself seven thousand who had not bowed the knee to Baal. Sennacherib's army marched to the walls of Jerusalem and then was smitten by the angel of the Lord.

> Like the leaves of the forest when Summer is green,
> That host with their banners at sunset were seen:
> Like the leaves of the forest when Autumn hath blown,
> That host on the morrow lay wither'd and strown.
>
> For the Angel of Death spread his wings on the blast,
> And breathed in the face of the foe as he pass'd;
> And the eyes of the sleepers wax'd deadly and chill,
> And their hearts but once heaved, and for ever grew still![1]

Jesus was crucified on a cross, but as soon as He was crucified He began to draw men to Him. Stephen was stoned. But Saul, who helped to stone him, was converted and became the apostle to the Gentiles. Herod Agrippa, grandson of Herod the Great, killed James the brother of John with the sword and put Peter in prison, intending to kill him also. But Peter was delivered by the angel of the Lord, while Herod was "eaten of worms, and gave up the ghost. But the word of God grew and multiplied."

Nero beheaded Paul; the Empire persecuted the church, but only to see the blood of the martyr become the seed of the church. A thousand heresies, false Christianities, false Christs

---

1. Lord Byron, "The Destruction of Sennacherib."

have arisen, and still arise, and still flourish; but the praying, witnessing, believing church is always preserved. After the battles of the ages, we hear with the new meaning those words that Christ spoke in the desert of Caesarea Philippi, "The gates of hell shall not prevail against it." No matter how great the rage, no matter how wild the fury, no matter how deep the invasion of the hosts of evil, always there has been that divine limit, "Hitherto shalt thou come, but no further: and here shall thy proud waves be stayed."

TEXT FOR THE TIMES

As perhaps never before, people have a deep fear for the welfare of humanity, of civilization, of Christianity itself. Never since the prophetic words were spoken by Christ Himself have so many people's hearts been failing them. Herods, such as we thought were long extinct, have arisen everywhere to take counsel against God and against His anointed, to say among themselves: "Let us . . . cast away their cords from us." All over the world we see a fierce and determined hostility to a way of life that is the result and blessing of Christianity. At present, the sweep and sway of these antichrists is indeed appalling, so appalling that we can hardly conceive of the resulting brutality, hatred, blasphemy, and vindictiveness.

In such an hour then, this Christmas text, "When Herod was dead," has new meaning. These Herods, like all the other Herods, will pass and die, be eaten of worms. But Christian (not world) civilization—belief in justice, in righteousness, in God—will survive and endure as it always has in the past. Kingdoms will be shaken down and removed, but we have the "kingdom that cannot be shaken." Our King is the only king who is invincible.

When we look at the world, when we look at history, and when we think of the future, we must remember the viewpoint of God, with whom a thousand years are as but one day. That is what Peter told the scoffers who had forgotten the doctrine and triumph of the Second Advent. Because all things "continue as they were from the beginning of the creation," they claimed that a divine intervention was preposterous, unthinkable. But they were ignorant of the fact, said Peter, that "one day is with the Lord as a thousand years, and a thousand years as one day." We must think in centuries, if we are going to think with God. If people who hate the truth, who disbelieve in Christ, forget that a thousand years with God are as but one day, we who believe in God must never forget it.

Sometimes this conflict between Herod and Jesus is localized in a single heart. Each one of us has within him or her a natural Herod who is opposed to Christ. He waits to resist in us every influence of God's Holy Spirit. He waits to destroy, if possible, every newborn purpose of repentance and of righteousness, of Christian love and faith. But "greater is he that is in you, than he that is in the world." Let Herod die! Let unbelief, hatred, wicked desire, fear, doubt, and despair—let them all die; but let the Eternal Child live. Let Christ "reign in your members."

4

THE DESTINY OF JESUS—SIMEON

Behold, this child is set for the fall and rising again of many
in Israel; and for a sign which shall be spoken against, . . . that
the thoughts of many hearts may be revealed (Luke 2:34–35).

I have never read any comment on it, but I take it for granted
that Raphael's great painting of Jesus and His mother in
the Dresden gallery, the so-called Sistine Madonna, is an at-
tempt to describe the thoughts and emotions of the mother
and her child at the presentation in the temple. Mary, listening
to the words of Simeon, presents, and yet holds back, her
child; her unfocused eyes seem to be filled with wonder and
awe as she sees far in the distance the strange destiny of the
child who rests in her arms.

Simeon was a just man and devout, one who waited for the
consolation of Israel, and to whom it had been revealed by the
Holy Spirit that he should not see death before he had seen
the Lord's Christ. He had come by the Spirit into the temple
when Joseph and Mary brought up Jesus to present him. By a
revelation he knew that this child was the Lord's Christ and,
taking Him up in his arms, he blessed Him.

If we had the gift of Simeon and could cast the horoscope of
a child and speak its destiny, the mother's face would be filled
with wonder and awe, perhaps also with dread, as she
contemplated the path of hardship, of sorrow, and of pain that
her child is to tread; or the career of crime that he will

accomplish; the days of loneliness, the hours of anguish, perhaps also deeds of dishonor and of shame. It is just as well that the future is veiled and that no Simeon can stand in our midst and sketch the future of a child as he did the future of the Divine Child who lay that day in Mary's arms. Yet every life is full of wonder, of mystery, of awe. What the people said on learning the circumstances of the birth of John the Baptist we can all say when we look into the face of a baby, "What manner of child shall this be!"

When he took the child in his arms, the devout Simeon blessed Joseph and spoke to Mary, the mother. If, a little before, Luke says that the *parents* brought in the child Jesus, as though Joseph were just as much a parent of the child as Mary, let it be noted how careful he is to say here that it was to Mary His mother that Simeon addressed himself when he declared the destiny of the child. "Behold, this child is set for the fall and rising again of many in Israel; and for a sign which shall be spoken against; (Yea, a sword shall pierce through thy own soul also,) that the thoughts of many hearts may be revealed."

In this statement of the destiny of Jesus there are three things said of Him, all of them strikingly illustrated and fulfilled in the life of Jesus, in the history of His church ever since, and in the lives and hearts of people today. First, Christ is to people either a blessing or a condemnation. Second, His presence, His truth, His church, will ever create opposition. And third, Christ is the revealer of the thoughts of the heart, the supreme touchstone of human nature.

CHRIST A BLESSING OR A CONDEMNATION

He is set for the fall and rising again of many in Israel. Christ either condemns people, or justifies them and saves them. In Him people are saved or lost. He is a stone of stumbling upon which they fall, or a rock by which they rise to life eternal.

Simeon, inspired by the Holy Spirit, said that Christ is "set," appointed or established, for the falling and rising again of many in Israel. He did not mean that Christ is sent by God to make people stumble and fall, but that stumbling and rising again will ever be the effect of His person and His truth as people encounter Him upon the pathway of life. In Christ there is no neutrality. People are either for Him or against Him. They rise through Him, or because of Him they fall.

We know how true this was during Christ's life upon earth. There were many who were offended in Him, many who stumbled and fell. The scribes, the Pharisees, the Sadducees, Herod, Pilate, Caiaphas, Judas—all of these men fell, whereas others rose. Many who stood high fell; many who were poor and humble were exalted. To some, His person and His doctrines present insuperable difficulties and make demands that arouse the bitter antagonism of the heart. The very righteousness of these demands, the reasonableness of them, only arouses the more the antagonism of human nature.

This is why it is a solemn and searching thing to be confronted with Christ in the Scriptures, in the proclamation of the church, in the lives of His followers. To have a duty presented to us, and then we refuse it; to have a higher path opened to us, and we decline it; to have a sin revealed to us, and we refuse to leave it or mourn over it—this is to stumble and to fall. But to obey, to change our lives, to repent, to believe—this is to rise to new levels of character.

It has become a fashion today to eulogize doubt and to praise doubters as superior minds and, presumably, superior characters. It is worthwhile remembering, therefore, that we have nothing of that in Christ or in the Scriptures. Christ makes it clear that the different attitudes of people toward Him are to be accounted for by differences in their hearts. He told them plainly that the reason they did not believe in Him and love Him was because the love of the Father was not in their hearts. They were not of the truth; therefore, they would not come to Him.

In the great doctrines of the Christian faith—the Incarnation, the Atonement, the Resurrection, the Holy Spirit, the present intercession of the Son of God, and His second coming to judge humans and angels—some find only an occasion for scorn and angry rejection, or they treat them as old wives' tales. But others rise upon these granite foundations of faith to holiness of life and to fellowship with God. They find them to be neither a stumbling block nor foolishness, but the power and the wisdom of God. How shall we account for this difference, this contrasting reaction to Christ and His Gospel? Not in environment, not in training, not in education, not in heredity; for those who have had the same training, environment, heredity, and education immediately part company in the presence of Christ, some stumbling upon Him and falling, others rising through faith and obedience to nobility and beauty of life. The reason is a difference in life, a difference in heart.

The last scene in the earthly life of Christ is a tragic demonstration of the way in which Christ divides among people. It was a prefiguration, too, of His influence upon human nature through all the ages. There He hung between the two thieves, both of whom at first reviled Him and cursed Him and mocked, while but one repented and said, "Lord, remember me when thou comest into thy kingdom." So Christ is set for the falling and rising again of many souls; so He divides among people. He is to some the savor of death to death, but to others the savor of life to life. It is this fact which gives an immense earnestness and solemnity to the preaching of Christ and His Gospel. No one can hear it without being made thereby either better or worse. It is the proclamation of life eternal to them that believe, the proclamation of death to them that reject Him.

CHRIST ALWAYS OPPOSED IN THE WORLD

"Behold, this child is set . . . for a sign which shall be spoken against." The angels, when they announced the birth of Christ, foretold only His glory and His triumph. It remained for the devout Simeon to tell the plain truth, that Christ, who had come in the beauty of holiness and innocence, the incarnation of divine love and pity and compassion, would be encompassed by hatred and enemies at every step in His earthly career, until at length the storm of human passion and anger would break over His head upon the cross.

There are many scenes in the history of the human race that are of a nature to undeceive those who will know nothing of human nature but its goodness and excellence. But the one chapter in the history of humanity that forever refutes such a definition of human nature is that chapter that relates for us the life and the death of Jesus Christ. There we learn what human nature is and to what lengths it will go. "This child is set . . . for a sign which shall be spoken against." We recall that some said He had a devil and others that He was mad, that men took up stones to stone Him, that they tried to throw Him over a precipice, that they betrayed Him and mocked Him and spat upon Him and crowned Him with thorns and crucified Him. When we reflect that we share the same nature as those men, then we come to understand how far the heart can go in its rebellion against God.

In how striking a manner the prediction of Simeon has been fulfilled. Wherever Christ, His cause, His church, His Gospel, His doctrines, His true disciples are, there Christ will be "spoken against." Wherever He is not spoken against, wherever His Gospel is not rejected and scorned but received with polite courtesy or dismissed with cool indifference, there you can be sure that it is not Christ who is preached and that what appears to be the Gospel is "another gospel: which is not another." Christ, the real Gospel, will always be a sign to be spoken against.

It is possible so to preach Christ that He will not be spoken against. You can leave out His claims to preexistence, deity, world dominion, and judgment; you can omit His stern demands upon believers; you can be silent as to the solitary and exclusive way of righteousness and salvation by faith in Him alone. All these things that are repugnant to the natural mind and heart of the individual you can leave out, but only to discover that Christ so preached is not a sign to be spoken against.

Paul tells us in his letter to the Galatians how people urged him to tone down the terms of redemption and tried to persuade him to say that, although people were saved by Christ, it was also necessary for them to observe certain Jewish laws and rites. But Paul refused to do so, for then would cease the "offense of the cross," that the sinner is saved only by faith in Christ. That, to Paul, was the power of the Gospel, the Gospel of which he was not ashamed, the Gospel in which he gloried. Nothing less than this seems now to be the question before the church. Shall the Gospel no longer be a stone of stumbling or a rock of rising—a sign to be spoken against or a truth to be embraced with rapture, love, and joy? Shall it cease to be the Gospel (good news) and become merely good advice?

CHRIST THE TOUCHSTONE OF THE HUMAN HEART

"That the thoughts of many hearts may be revealed." The one great purpose of our earthly probation is that God may know our hearts. Not that in His omniscience He cannot know and see what is in the heart now, or what the heart will do in the years to come; rather, that by the experience of life, by the use or abuse of its opportunities, everyone should write a description of his character. This, we are told, was His purpose in His dealings with Israel. "Thou shalt remember all the way which the Lord thy God led thee these forty years in the wilderness, to humble thee, and to prove thee, to know what was in thine heart, whether thou wouldst keep his commandments, or no." The life of the heart is the critical thing. Out of the heart are the issues of life. Not what goes into one, but what comes out of one's heart defiles one. If people do not love Christ, it is because the love of God is not in their hearts. With the heart, a person believes to life. It is therefore in harmony with this great fact of life that Christ is declared to be the one who, above all others, tests the heart and reveals its secrets and its thoughts.

We can see how true this was during the life of Christ upon earth. There was something in Him and in His truth that awakened latent evil and latent good. The scribes, the Pharisees, the Sadducees, Herod, Pilate, Caiaphas, and Judas, when brought before Christ, revealed themselves, their anger, hypocrisy, blasphemy, bitterness, enmity to good, their hatred, and their treason. Others brought before Christ had discovered in themselves that which God delights to find: Mary, her gratitude; the publican, his penitence; the Magdalene, her love; the centurion, his great faith; the thief on the cross, his penitence. So Christ has ever been revealing, uncovering, discovering what is in the heart. The same sun that shines upon the earth today ripens the wheat and also the tares. The same sun that scatters the darkness and dissipates the clouds also draws out of the earth its noxious mists and vapors. So Christ acts upon the hearts of human beings.

In Christ the one great, decisive, searching thing is His remedy for sin—forgiveness through faith, cleansing through His blood. How that test at once reveals, searches a person's heart! When we say that Christ searches the heart, reveals its secret thoughts, we do not mean that in one individual He discovers only that which is unworthy, for all have sinned and come short of the glory of God, but that in one He discovers a refusal of God's will and plan, and in the other a humble and grateful acceptance of it. In one, He finds self-righteousness; in the other, the publican's cry, "God be merciful to me a sinner."

Let the Cross be plunged down today into your heart. What is the reaction to it? People speak of salvation by character. Yes, if by that they mean the Gospel standard of character, the Gospel's method of ascertaining the true character of a person's heart; for the supreme test of character is the soul's reaction to the offer of Christ crucified. The acceptance or the rejection of that shows the moral drift of a person's nature; nothing that he can say or do, good or bad, is of the least significance as compared with that acceptance or that rejection.

When Sir Walter Raleigh was led to the block, his executioner asked him if his head lay right. Raleigh answered, "It matters little, my friend, how the head lies, provided the heart is right." Here in the presence of God, here before Him to whom are revealed the secrets of all hearts, here before the cross of mercy and of love, what does your heart speak? How does your heart lie?

5

AN AUTUMN BLOOMING—JAMES, THE BROTHER OF OUR LORD

He was seen of James (1 Cor. 15:7).

I f I had known that Lincoln was such a great man, there are many things that he said that I might have set down," wrote Whitney, one of Lincoln's biographers, in a book of memories. Yet he lived close to Lincoln for weeks at a time and did not recognize his greatness. James lived close to Jesus for many years but did not know He was great.

The Gospels have no record of this resurrection appearance of Jesus. We find it in Paul's catalog of the appearances of Jesus after His resurrection. It is, therefore, one of the three appearances of Christ to individuals. He appeared to Peter, to Mary of Magdala, and to James. In a way, this appearance to James is the most significant of all three. We might have expected that Jesus would appear to Mary, who so mourned Him. "Blessed are they that mourn: for they shall be comforted." I wonder if Mary thought of that and if she recalled this saying of Jesus when she heard Him call her by name that morning by the empty sepulcher? We might have expected, too, that He would appear to Peter, who had so cruelly and shamefully denied Him but had repented and wept bitterly. But James was His own brother, and one of the brothers who did not believe upon Him. The appearances to the other disciples and friends were to convince them that Jesus had risen from the dead. But this appearance to James, seemingly the only one to an unbeliever, was for the purpose of changing him from an unbeliever into a disciple.

The James that Paul mentions has generally been identified as the brother of the Lord. The Gospels tell us that Jesus had four brothers: James, Joseph, Simon, and Judas. It tells us also that they thought He was "beside himself." "Neither did his brethren believe in him." This does not necessarily mean that they did not respect Him or did not love Him as a brother, but that they rejected the claims He had made to being the Messiah of Israel. They had remonstrated with Him on that point. They had warned Him not to go up to Jerusalem. Nevertheless, they must have regretted His violent and shameful death as a malefactor on the cross. It was then, to one of these brothers— and since James is always mentioned first in the list, probably the oldest of them—that Jesus made His appearance after His resurrection.

We can imagine James at work in the carpenter shop at Nazareth. Perhaps he was saying to himself: "If only our brother had taken our advice and abandoned His foolish idea that He was the Messiah! We all warned Him. But He would have His own way. He went up to Jerusalem where His enemies were, and now they have put Him to death. How different it might have been with Him!" Then he hears a voice calling him by name, "James!" And there before him, just as he had known Him in the flesh, stands Jesus! I can well imagine, too, how Jesus would say to James that He had appeared to him in a special way in order that He might win him as a disciple. He probably spoke of the other brothers also—Joseph, and Simon, and Judas—and His sisters. He must have asked James to tell them that He loved them and that He had risen from the dead.

No one could claim that this was a supposed appearance to one of the disciples and followers of Jesus who had hoped, and expected, that even after Christ had been crucified He would rise again from the dead. That was what Renan said of Mary Magdalene: she was hoping and longing to see Jesus; in the garden, instead of supposing Jesus to be the gardener, as John tells us, she must have taken the gardener for Jesus. And so, out of hallucination, says Renan, came the story of the Resurrection. But hardheaded James was one of those four brothers who had not believed on Jesus. He had never taken Him as the Messiah and had never expected that He would survive death and rise from the grave. Yet Jesus appears to James and turns him into a believer, and a great believer. He becomes the leader and bishop of the church at Jerusalem, recognized by Paul as one of the "pillars" of the church. He becomes the author of the letter that bears his name. In that letter he signs himself "James, a servant [literally, "slave"] of God and of the Lord Jesus Christ." He becomes the man who is noted for the emphasis that he placed upon a Christian life—the man who says that "faith without works is dead" and that if we have faith, we must show it by our lives, our good works. That this change was made in a brother so unbelieving and so opposed as James was to Jesus is a great and striking evidence of the fact of the Resurrection. Just as the change in Paul from the chief persecutor and enemy of Jesus to His greatest apostle can be accounted for only by the resurrection appearance of Jesus to Paul, so the transformation and conversion of James can be accounted for only on the ground of the truth of what Paul relates, "He was seen of James."

JESUS RECOGNIZES THE BONDS OF THE FAMILY LIFE

The most touching instance of that recognition, of course, occurred when Jesus was expiring on the cross. Seeing His mother and that disciple whom He loved "standing by," Christ said to His mother, "Behold thy son!" and to John, "Behold thy mother!" But here, too, in this appearance to James we have a tender and beautiful recognition of the family relationship.

We cannot be altogether certain as to how Jesus used the word *brethren*. When He was risen and appeared to the women who had gone to the grave, He told them, "Go tell my brethren that they go into Galilee, and there shall they see me." Likewise when He appeared to Mary of Magdala, He said to her, "Go to my brethren, and say to them, I ascend to my Father, and your Father; and to my God, and your God." It may well be that by "brethren" Jesus here means, not the whole company of His disciples, but His own four brothers: James, Joseph, Simon, and Judas. If so, there is something very moving and tender in the fact that after His resurrection He thinks first of all about those unbelieving brothers. By so doing, and by this appearance to James, He teaches us the obligation we owe to our own flesh and blood, both for this world and for the world to come. The first thing Andrew did when he found Christ was to find his own brother, Peter, and bring him to Christ. And here, after the Resurrection, we see Jesus seeking out that unbelieving brother and bringing him into the kingdom.

UNRECOGNIZED GREATNESS

For thirty years James lived near Jesus; for many years, in the same home and in the same town. Others came to believe on Jesus as the Son of God and the Messiah and left all to follow Him. But not so James. He thought Jesus was "beside himself" and altogether mistaken in His ideas. It took this special appearance after the Resurrection to open the eyes of James to the greatness and beauty of Christ.

In his famous story "The Great Stone Face," Hawthorne tells of a mountain where the rocks had been so cast up by past convulsions that they resembled a human countenance, a face of great dignity and strength, of beauty and compassion. If the observer were too near, the outlines of the face were lost; but, standing at a distance, one could see the great arch of the forehead, the vast lips, the deep eyes.

In the valley at the foot of the mountain, there was a lad who liked to sit by the side of his mother and gaze on the Stone Face. One day he said to his mother that he wished the lips of the Stone Face would speak, for if the face were human, he would love him. The mother told the child that perhaps this might happen. According to a legend dating back to the time of the Indians, one who had been born in that valley was destined one day to become the greatest and noblest of all, and his face would have an exact resemblance to the Stone Face. After hearing the legend, the boy regarded the Stone Face as a teacher and an inspirer. The vast countenance seemed to smile upon the child and to encourage him in his dreams.

At length the report spread through the valley that a man who had been born there was coming back to end his days at the foot of the mountain. He was one who had achieved great wealth. He had the Midas touch and everything that he touched turned to gold. The Arctic wastes, the mountain forests, the ocean depths, the rivers of the tropics—all brought him gold, until at length he had so much that it would have taken a hundred years to count his wealth. When he decided to go back to his native valley and spend his last days there, he ordered built for himself a great marble mansion. At length the day came when he appeared in the valley. When the inhabitants saw him, they said that the ancient prophecy had come true. "Here is the very image of the Stone Face!" But when the rich man, driving by in his carriage, leaned out for a moment to toss some pennies to a poor family, what the expectant boy saw was the sordid face of an old man, with a low brow, sharp eyes, and thin lips—a face that was yellow and covered with wrinkles. The boy walked sadly away, for he knew that this face was not that on the majestic mountain.

The years went by, and the boy had become a young man. Again the rumor spread that the one who was going to fulfill the prophecy would soon appear in the valley. This time it was a man who had been born in the valley and who had won renown as a military commander. Weary of military life and campaigns, he was now coming back to end his days in the valley where he was born. The inhabitants gave him a great welcome and met him with cavalcades and parades and banners. A banquet was spread for him in the grove, and the people who assembled could see, far in the distance, the stone face of the mountain. Many of them, looking upon the iron countenance of the old soldier, exclaimed, " 'Tis the same face to a hair! Now the prophecy has been fulfilled!" But when the commander arose to speak, the young man, who was still looking for the fulfillment of the prophecy, saw a worn and weather-beaten face. It was indeed expressive of iron will and determination, but there was nothing of the wisdom, calmness, and sympathy of the Stone Face. Again the youth was disappointed.

More years passed by, and the lad was now a man in middle life. Once again the rumor spread that a man was to appear in the valley who would fulfill the ancient prophecy, a great man, and the exact resemblance of the Stone Face. This man had been born in the valley and had become a lawyer and a politician. He had the gift of eloquence, the power of words—a greater power than that of wealth or the sword. He could make wrong seem right and right seem wrong, and with his words he could create a fog that obscured natural daylight. He was now a candidate for the presidency, and during the campaign he resolved to visit his native valley.

He was met by societies and organizations and martial music and conducted to a grove where a banquet was spread for him. Overhead were hung portraits of the Stone Face and of the celebrated orator and statesman. The natives this time were sure that the prophecy had been fulfilled and exclaimed one to another, "It is the old Stone Face itself!" And indeed, at first glimpse, there was something about the statesman's face that looked like the countenance of the mountain. It had the massive brow, the expressive lips, the noble nose, and the cavern-like eyes. But in the eyes one detected a weariness and a gloom, as of a child who had outgrown its playthings, as of a life that, despite its high performance, was vague and empty because no high purpose had endowed it with reality. Once again the boy, now a man, was disappointed.

Years passed, and now the boy was an old man. He had become noted in his valley for his deeds of kindness, his words of wisdom and of grace. Even from outside the valley, visitors would come to see him and to hear him and went away astonished at his wisdom. And when they were leaving the valley, and looked on the Stone Face, they all felt that they had seen a face somewhere that resembled the mountain face, but they wondered where it was. Among these was a poet whose verses had found their way to this philosopher of the valley. When the old man read the words of the poet it seemed as if they echoed all beauty and truth.

One day the poet came to visit the philosopher. As he listened to the man of the valley, it seemed to him that never man spoke as did this untrained philosopher of the wilderness. As they talked together, the old man looked earnestly into the poet's face and asked him who he was. The poet laid his hand on the book of verse that the old man held and said, "I am the man who wrote these words." Again, and more earnestly, the philosopher looked into the poet's face and then turned to look at the Great Stone Face. As he did so, a look of disappointment and sorrow came into his countenance. The poet asked him why this sorrow. The old man explained that all his life he had waited for the coming of the man whose face would be the exact resemblance of the Stone Face and who would be greatest and noblest of all, and he had hoped that the poet would fulfill the prophecy.

The poet then told him it was not strange that he was disappointed. "But," the old man said, "are these thoughts not divine which you have expressed?" The poet replied, "They have a strain of the Divinity in them, and you can hear in them the far-off echo of the heavenly song; but my life has not corresponded with my thoughts. I have lacked faith in the grandeur, the beauty, and the goodness of my own dreams." As he said this the poet's eyes were filled with tears, and likewise the eyes of the valley philosopher.

That night at sunset, as was his custom, the old man of the valley delivered to his neighbors a discourse on life and its meaning. As they were listening to him they could see in the distance the Great Stone Face with mists around it. As he looked at the Stone Face, and then at the face of the old man who was addressing them, the poet exclaimed: "Behold! He himself is the likeness of the Great Stone Face!" Then all the people looked and they saw that what he said was true. The prophecy was fulfilled! For years they had been waiting for some famous person to come from afar who would perfectly resemble the Great Stone Face and thus fulfill the ancient prophecy; and lo, they found him in one of their neighbors with whom they had lived in the sequestered valley all their lives!

Thus often it is in this life. The beautiful story shows, not only how people become what they contemplate and how the soul is dyed the color of its thoughts, but how easy it is to live side by side with greatness and nobility of character and yet never see it. That was so with James, the brother of the Lord. He lived for thirty years with Jesus; it was only when Jesus appeared to him after His death and the Resurrection that he saw in Him the Son of God, the Savior of the world, and his own redeemer.

Cherish what is dear to you while it is near. Beautiful souls are not far from you.

> Like birds, whose beauties languish half conceal'd,
> Till, mounted on the wing, their glossy plumes
> Expanded, shine with azure, green and gold;
> How blessings brighten as they take their flight.[1]

---

1. Edward Young.

6

RUINED BY PROSPERITY—UZZIAH

He was marvelously helped, till he was strong. But when he
was strong, his heart was lifted up to his destruction: for he
transgressed against the Lord his God (2 Chron. 26:15–16).

U zziah is one of the most noteworthy of the kings of Judah.
He has two names in the Bible. In the book of Kings he is
called Azariah but in the book of Chronicles, Uzziah. It is by
the latter that he is best known. He came to the throne when
he was only sixteen years of age. He reigned for fifty-two
years, and his reign was almost the longest and, in certain
respects, the most glorious in the history of the kingdom. He
began his reign with great promise. It is written that he sought
God in the days of Zechariah, the high priest, and that as long
as he sought the Lord, God made him to prosper. Yet this
long and glorious reign ended in tragedy.

UZZIAH—KING AND CONQUEROR

When he ascended the throne, the young Uzziah revealed
splendid traits and high ability. The fortunes and the defenses
of the kingdom were then at a low ebb. The first thing he did
was to subdue the Edomites, the congenital enemies of Israel,
and to take the port of Eloth on the Red Sea, thus reviving the
commerce which had flourished in the days of Solomon. Next
he smote the Philistines, capturing their strongholds of Gath

and Ashdod. Two other longtime enemies of Israel, always a thorn in the side of the nation, were also subdued—the Ammonites and the Arabians. These conquests gave Uzziah great renown and made his name feared as far as the gates of Egypt.

At home he restored the defenses of Jerusalem, building strong towers on the walls to resist a besieging army. He also invented military engines, like the catapults of the Romans, to hurl arrows and darts and to cast stones down upon a besieging army. He organized a great standing army of 307,000 men and had a special crack troop, like David's mighty men, except that Uzziah's numbered not 600, but 2,600.

Uzziah was also a great agriculturalist—an asset for any leader of the people. It is written that he "loved husbandry." He cultivated vineyards in the mountains and developed and operated cattle ranches in the low country and on the plains. For their defense and sustenance he built towers in the desert and sank many wells.

Such, then, was Uzziah until his fall—God-fearing, a great ruler, a great general and conqueror, a great inventor, a great agriculturalist, a great organizer. It is written of him that "his name spread far abroad; for he was marvelously helped, till he was strong."

THE FALL OF UZZIAH

But when Uzziah had become strong, "his heart was lifted up to his destruction." Not content with his fame as a warrior, inventor, and agriculturalist, he arrogated the sacred functions of the priesthood. He went into the temple to burn incense upon the golden altar of incense, which stood just outside the great crimson veil of the temple. Like the Roman emperors, he wanted to be the pontiff also, the head of religion.

He would have carried out this sacrilege had it not been for the courageous high priest Azariah, the successor to the one who had had such influence upon the early life of Uzziah. This fearless priest, taking with him a number of other priests, followed the king into the temple. Just as Uzziah was about to offer the incense on the altar, Azariah withstood him to his face, saying: "It is not for thee, Uzziah, to burn incense unto the Lord. This is the work and ministry of the priests, the sons of Aaron, who are consecrated to this office. Go out of the sanctuary, for thou hast trespassed; neither shall it be for thine honor from the Lord God."

This protest and rebuke by the priest enraged the king, who was holding the censer in his hand to burn incense. From the record we infer that he was ready to strike the high priest with his censer. But before he could strike the high priest or offer the incense, lo, leprosy rose up in his forehead! When the priests saw that he had become a leper, they thrust him out of the holy house. Since no leper could reign as king, he was removed from his throne and spent the rest of his days in a lazar house. "And Uzziah the king was a leper unto the day of his death."

That, then, is the story of Uzziah. "He was marvelously helped, till he was strong. But when he was strong, his heart was lifted up to his destruction: for he transgressed against the Lord his God."

The Peril of Prosperity

The tragedy of Uzziah tells us of the danger lurking in success. Everyone wants to succeed. Everyone wants to exert influence in his or her chosen and appointed place. But there is a peril in success; for often, as in the case of Uzziah, worldly success lifts one's heart up so that one loses one's humble trust in God.

Waiting once for an installation service to commence at a church in New Jersey, I fell into conversation with an elder in the church. He had been most prosperous in business, but recently had suffered serious reverses. After telling me of these reverses he said, "I am glad that I failed, for I was getting away from God." It takes humility to keep a person safe when he or she has power, riches, or worldly success. Always we must ask for humble hearts.

The great preacher George Whitefield, just before he began his sermon one day in his Tottingham Road Chapel in London, was handed a note which read: "The prayers of this congregation are desired for a young man who has become heir to an immense fortune and who feels much need of grace to keep him humble in the midst of his riches." In too many cases, people rising to high places have forgotten to make the prayer of that young man.

Prosperity is always dangerous. It inclines a person's heart to pride. At the zenith of his power and ruler of a world empire, Nebuchadnezzar boasted, "Is not this great Babylon, that I have built?" God's answer was to drag him down from his throne and turn him out into the fields, where he ate grass like an ox until he learned that there was a God in heaven.

In his grand farewell address to the children of Israel, recorded in the book of Deuteronomy, Moses warned the people against the dangers of prosperity. He had told them of the good land, the Promised Land, to which God would bring them according to His promise, and when they reached that land, he told them to "bless the Lord thy God for the good land which he hath given thee." Then he warned them to beware lest in the day of prosperity and success they should overlook their part in this promise.

> Beware that thou forget not the Lord thy God, in not keeping his commandments, and his judgments, and his statutes, which I command thee this day: lest when thou hast eaten and art full, and hast built goodly houses, and dwelt therein; and when thy herds and thy flocks multiply, and thy silver and thy gold is multiplied, and all that thou hast is multiplied; then thine heart be lifted up, and thou forget the Lord thy God, which brought thee forth out of the land of Egypt, from the house of bondage; . . . and thou say in thine heart, My power and the might of mine hand hath gotten me this wealth.

What is true of the nation is true of the individual. What Moses describes there, and what afterward took place—the people of Israel forgetting that it was the Lord their God who brought them out of the land of Egypt and out of the house of bondage, and thinking that their own power and might had secured them prosperity in the promised land—that very thing happened to King Uzziah. He forgot that it was the Lord his God who had so wonderfully helped him; he assumed that he had succeeded by his own power and could safely defy God's commandments. The prophet Hosea strikes the same note when, speaking for God, he says: "Their heart was exalted; therefore have they forgotten me." And again, "As they were increased, so they sinned against me."

Although he did not so completely flout God's will as did Uzziah, another great king of Judah, Hezekiah, in the day of his prosperity let his pride turn him from God. God had delivered him in a wonderful way from the might of the Assyrian despot Sennacherib. God had also spared the life of Hezekiah when he was sick to death and had sent the shadow back for him ten degrees on the dial, granting him fifteen more years of life. But as the chronicler says, "Hezekiah rendered not again according to the benefit done unto him; for his heart was lifted up." Instead of acting in humility and gratitude to God, he received the ambassadors of the king of Babylon as if they were the friends of his nation and showed them all his riches and treasures and the splendor of his kingdom. For that pride and presumption Isaiah pronounced upon Hezekiah the judgment of God, telling him that all these treasures and possessions which he had so proudly shown to the ambassadors of Babylon would one day be carried thither, and nothing would be left of them in Jerusalem. Thus the Bible, page after page, rings the changes on this great and important truth, that the natural tendency of the human heart is to forget its obligation to God in the day of prosperity.

During a summer vacation a minister from the city went to worship in a Pennsylvania county town. After the service he fell into conversation with an official of the small church. Learning the city where the minister lived, the elder asked about a college classmate of his who as a young man had gone to this city and entered upon the practice of law. He spoke of the brilliance of his intellect and the expectations that were entertained for his success in life. When they were classmates together, he related, the college was shaken with a revival, and this youth was the leader of all in participating in the meetings and in pressing the claims of Christ upon others. He wondered if his old classmate had kept up that testimony. He wondered if he was in the church, and took an active part in its work.

The minister knew the man and could tell his story. When

he first came to the city, he at once associated himself with the church and became a teacher in the Sabbath school. As the years went by, he rose rapidly in his profession and met with great success, until at length he held a high post in the government. But as his material success increased, his religious life declined. At length he was separated completely from the church. He had risen to a high place and had won great success as a lawyer, but, for all one knew, God now was not in all his thoughts. The last the minister had heard of him was his appearance as counsel for the liquor interests when a bill for prohibition was before the state legislature.

Human nature does not change through the ages. All that the Bible says about the danger of prosperity, without remembrance that it is God who helps us to the prosperity, is true today. There is no doubt whatever that in every field of life—business, manufacturing, education, public life, and the arts—there are those who once were earnest and faithful in the church and in the work of Christ but who have drifted completely out of that association. They were marvelously helped until they were strong; when they were strong, their hearts were lifted up to their destruction, and they transgressed against the Lord their God.

One of the old saints used to pray, "Lord, guard me against a departing heart." The human heart naturally declines from and departs from God. As the psalmist said, our souls cleave to the dust. In prosperity, and in adversity too, may God guard us all against a "departing heart."

7

TWO DESTINIES— CAIN AND ABEL

Cain rose up against Abel his brother, and slew him (Gen. 4:8).

The book of Genesis is a book of beginnings. It throws a flashlight on the early history of humanity. It is a book of first things. In this fourth chapter of Genesis we have the first father, the first mother, the first birth, the first son, the first altar, the first murder, and the first death.

Here at the beginning of human history, the stream of humanity is divided into two kinds of people—people with different characters and different destinies. In his poem "The Two Streams," Oliver Wendell Holmes deals with this mysterious difference in character and in destiny. He describes two rivers formed by the rainfall on a mountain, one flowing eastward, the other westward:

> Behold the rocky wall
> That down its sloping sides
>   Pours the swift rain-drops, blending, as they fall,
> In rushing river-tides!

Yon stream, whose sources run
Turned by a pebble's edge,
   Is Athabasca, rolling toward the sun
Through the cleft in mountain-ledge.

The slender rill had strayed,
But for the slanting stone,
   To evening's ocean, with the tangled braid
Of foam-flecked Oregon.

So from the heights of Will
Life's parting stream descends,
   And, as a moment turns its slender rill,
Each widening torrent bends,—

From the same cradle's side,
From the same mother's knee,—
   One to long darkness and the frozen tide,
One to the Peaceful Sea!

The Bible does not permit us to forget the tragedy of Abel and Cain. When Jesus pronounced judgment on the scribes and Pharisees, He said, "That upon you may come all the righteous blood shed upon the earth, from the blood of righteous Abel unto the blood of Zacharias." In his first letter, John writes, "Ye heard from the beginning, that we should love one another. Not as Cain, who was of that wicked one, and slew his brother." And in the letter to the Hebrews, the immortal roll call of the heroes of faith commences with Abel: "By faith Abel offered unto God a more excellent sacrifice than Cain." In that same book, in a grand chapter that sets forth the high privilege and the noble destiny of believers, the author says: "Ye are come unto . . . God the Judge of all, and to the spirits of just men made perfect, and to Jesus the mediator of the new covenant, and to the blood of sprinkling, that speaketh better things than that of Abel." In his fiery one-chapter epistle, Jude, describing the evil people and the unbelievers of his day, writes: "Woe unto them! for they have gone in the way of Cain."

Two Brothers

The tragedy of Cain and Abel is a tragedy of two brothers. Some of the most stirring incidents of the Bible center around brothers: Cain and Abel; Isaac and Ishmael, the son of the bondwoman; Jacob and Esau; Absalom and Amnon; James and John; Peter and Andrew; Joseph and his brethren. Some of these biographies are sad and tragic, some of them beautiful; all are timeless in their instruction.

That was a great day for the first man and the first woman when Cain was born. If, after the lapse of long ages, a child born this morning brings a thrill of joy to its father and mother, then what must have been the joy and wonder in the hearts of Adam and Eve when they looked upon the face of the first child and realized that they too were creators, that they had made a contribution to the stream of life which began to flow that day in Cain and is still flowing. Great was the joy of the first mother. She realized that there was a divine gift and a divine purpose in the birth of her child; for she called him Cain and said, "I have gotten a man from the Lord." Perhaps, too, there was something more than joy and wonder. Perhaps when Eve looked upon her babe and confessed that she had gotten him with the help of God, she recalled the promise of God spoken after the Fall, how the seed of the woman would bruise the head of the serpent. "Perhaps," Eve thought, "my child will cancel and recall the curse which has fallen upon us."

When her second son was born she called him Abel, which means "breath," "vanity." Why did she give Abel that name? Was it because he was a frail child and she feared that even a breath might take him from her? Or was it because she had some forelook, some premonition, that great sorrow would come into her life because of what would happen to this second child?

In our imagination we can follow the infancy and childhood of those two brothers. Perhaps, who knows, before they had lived many years their mother noted differences in their personality and character. When they reached adulthood one became a tiller of the soil, a farmer; the other, a shepherd: humanity's two oldest occupations.

Just when the command was given to build an altar and

make a sacrifice, we know not. Perhaps it arose out of the instinct and desire of people to worship. To that altar Cain brought the firstfruits of the field, and Abel, the firstfruits of his flock. "The Lord had respect unto Abel and to his offering: but unto Cain and to his offering he had not respect." Why this difference? Why was the offering of Abel acceptable to God and the offering of Cain not acceptable?—certainly not because of a difference in the offerings that they brought. Both the fruits of the field and the firstlings of the flock come from God. Each brother brought that which was natural for him. There is no reason to think that each one did not bring the best of what he had.

The difference is to be found, not in the offering, but in those who made the offering. Just what that was we cannot be sure. If God rejected the offering of Cain, it must have been because there was something wrong in the heart of Cain when he brought his offering. Already there may have been enmity and jealousy toward his righteous brother. All we are told is what the verse in Hebrews tells us, that "by faith Abel offered unto God a more excellent sacrifice than Cain." Faith in what? Faith in God, and faith that the offering he brought would be acceptable to God and would bring God's blessing upon him.

GOD'S WARNINGS

When Cain's sacrifice was rejected he was very angry, and his countenance fell. For the first time the shadow of anger and hate darkened the human countenance. God was very patient with Cain; He expostulated with him and warned him: "Why art thou wroth? and why is thy countenance fallen? If thou doest well, shalt thou not be accepted? and if thou doest not well, sin lieth at the door. And unto thee shall be his desire." There, for the first time, is spoken that terrible word "sin," which henceforth sounds its ominous note all through the Bible.

God warned Cain, who already had displeased God by the spirit in which he brought his offering and by his anger, against future sin. He said to him: "If thou doest not well, sin lieth [literally, "croucheth"] at the door." What a picture of sin and temptation that is! If you and I had ever seen a wild beast—a tiger or a leopard—watching us, crouching, its body low to the ground, preparing to make its cruel spring, we could never forget it. Sin, God tells Cain, is like that crouching beast. Sin is watching him and waiting for him and ready to leap upon him at the first opportunity. Sin desires to have him. "Unto thee shall be his desire."

What God said to Cain is the second sermon that God preached to humans. The first was when He talked with the man and the woman after their fall. Here he warns Cain against the danger of future sin. Thus this sermon of God, how sin crouches at the door awaiting its chance, is one that warns us all. Alas, how many have spurned God's warnings as Cain did. Balaam was warned, but in vain; Solomon was warned, but in vain; Judas was warned, but in vain; Peter was warned, but in vain. God does not let people go down without warning.

Now we come to the first crime and the first murder. Centuries afterward, James gives us the natural history of sin and the consequences of sin, when he says: "Every man is tempted, when he is drawn away of his own lust, and enticed. Then when lust hath conceived, it bringeth forth sin: and sin, when it is finished, bringeth forth death." Here we see the "finish" of sin; that is, death. Here, too, we see the sequence of sin: first, anger; then, envy, hate, and murder.

John tells us that Cain slew his brother because of envy and jealousy—"Because his own works were evil, and his brother's righteous." This was the first, but not the last, fatal blow that jealousy struck. How many hearts it has broken; how many homes it has blasted; how many brothers and sisters, fathers and mothers, and friends it has alienated and separated. The history of humankind gives no occasion for revising the verdict of the Song of Solomon: "Jealousy is cruel as the grave: the coals thereof are coals of fire, which hath a most vehement flame."

Oh! beware, my lord, of jealousy;
It is the green-eyed monster which doth mock the meat it feeds on.[1]

---

1. Shakespeare, *Merchant of Venice*, 3.2.

How soon following God's warning the struggle between Cain and Abel took place we are not told. It may have been one day, or many days. But one day when they were in the field Cain "talked with Abel his brother." About what did he talk with him? Probably about Abel's accepted sacrifice and the rejected sacrifice of Cain. The more Cain talked, the angrier he became, until at length he lifted a stone or club and struck Abel down. Lord Byron's great drama of Cain represents him as being amazed at the silence of Abel. Cain was looking for the first time on the face of death and pleading with Abel to speak to him, asking, "Who makes me brotherless?" But there is no suggestion in the narrative of the Bible that Cain did anything of the sort. Instead, we read of his hardheartedness and defiance. The Lord spoke to Cain, saying, "Where is Abel thy brother?" Cain pretended ignorance of the whereabouts of Abel. "I know not," he said. "Am I my brother's keeper? I have something else to do than to run about to see where Abel is or what he is doing." Did Cain think, we wonder, that God did not know where Abel was and what had happened to him, his body lying perhaps in some shallow grave or hidden in the bushes? Now Cain learns that his deed cannot be concealed from God; now he hears the inevitable sentence upon sin, how the "wages of sin is death."

THE WAGES OF SIN

God said to Cain: "Now art thou cursed from the earth, which hath opened her mouth to receive thy brother's blood from thy hand; when thou tillest the ground, it shall not henceforth yield unto thee her strength; a fugitive and a vagabond shalt thou be in the earth." Cain had made an enemy not only of God, but of the earth, which had opened its mouth to receive the blood of the murdered Abel. He learns now that when he killed his brother he killed himself—killed his peace of mind. If only the blow that he struck his brother had put an end to it! But that was not the end.

"If it were done when 'tis done!" But sin is never done! Cain awakens now to remorse and dread and fear. Conscience makes a coward of him. His fear is that whoever sees him will slay him.

> My punishment is greater than I can bear. Behold, thou hast driven me out this day from the face of the earth; and from thy face shall I be hid; and I shall be a fugitive and a vagabond in the earth; and it shall come to pass, that every one that findeth me shall slay me.

God had pronounced the judgment and punishment upon Cain. He was to be a fugitive and a vagabond thenceforth in his journey; but still more so in his mind, in his soul, for there is no rest to the wicked. Yet God, although He judges sin and punishes sin, is also a God of mercy. He took steps to protect Cain from human vengeance. It was long afterward that God said it, but here He *acts* it: "Vengeance is mine; I will repay, saith the Lord." Instead of handing Cain over to human vengeance, God protected him from it. He "set a mark upon Cain," lest any finding him should kill him. The "brand of Cain" is one of the most familiar of sayings, applied to the murderer in every age. But this is a gross misuse of that incident. The mark that God put upon Cain was not a mark to show people that he was a murderer and guilty of death but rather a sign of mercy—some mysterious token that protected him from human wrath. Yet Cain could not be protected from himself. A person's own heart is his or her worst enemy, his or her most inexorable judge.

Cain "went out from the presence of the Lord." Those two words, "went out," tell the sad and changeless story of sin. Adam and Eve sinned and went out from the Garden; Cain sinned and "went out from the presence of the Lord"; Jacob sinned against his brother, Esau, and his father and went out from his father's house; Absalom sinned when he slew his brother and went out from his father's house and his native land; Peter sinned when he denied his Lord and "went out, and wept bitterly"; the Prodigal Son sinned and went out, and down, into the far country; Judas sinned, and when he had received the sop at the Lord's Supper, "went . . . out: and it was night."

When Cain went out from the presence of the Lord, he preached the first great sermon on the wages of sin. Sin separates one from one's friends. Here it broke up the first family. The real separation among friends and families is not the separation of sickness or death, but the separation of sin. When Judas went out that night from the Lord's Supper, I wonder if he paused for a moment and, looking up at the candlelit window of the Upper Chamber, said to himself, "I have separated myself from my friends and from my Lord."

Sin separates one from oneself and from one's peace of mind. A person becomes a fugitive from his or her own conscience. So forever is it true, "He that sinneth against [God] wrongeth his own soul." Byron missed the idea when he put regret and remorse into the mind and speech of Cain immediately after he had murdered his brother. But he did not miss it when he described the departure of Cain from the presence of the Lord, into the land of Nod. After he says farewell to the body of Abel, Cain takes his wife, Adah, and their children and starts eastward from Eden.

> Eastward from Eden will eve take our way;
> 'Tis the most desolate, and suits my steps.

His wife bids farewell to the murdered Abel, "Peace be with him!" Cain answers, "But not with *me!*"

THE REDEMPTION OF CAIN

In the writer's great passage in Hebrews, where he speaks of the privilege and ultimate destiny of believers in Jesus and contrasts the high privilege of those who live in this day of grace with those who lived under the law, he says:

> Ye are come unto Mount Sion, and unto the city of the living God, the heavenly Jerusalem, and to an innumerable company of angels, to the general assembly and church of the first-born, which are written in heaven, and to God the Judge of all, and to the spirits of just men made perfect, and to Jesus the mediator of the new covenant, and to the blood of sprinkling, that speaketh better things than that of Abel.

"Better things than [the blood] of Abel." How true that is! In the deep tragedy of Cain and Abel, the singular, and in some ways the most impressive, thing is the silence of Abel.

Abel never speaks. It is only after he has been slain and the earth has opened its mouth to drink his blood that Abel begins to speak. "The blood of Abel, thy brother, crieth to me from the ground." The blood of Abel spoke of sin and its punishment, but the blood of Jesus speaks of forgiveness. The blood of Abel spoke of hate, but the blood of Jesus speaks of love. The blood of Abel spoke of separation—Cain going out from the presence of the Lord, but the blood of Jesus speaks of reconciliation. The blood of Abel spoke of fear; the blood of Jesus speaks of peace. The blood of Abel spoke of death, which is the wages of sin; the blood of Jesus speaks of eternal life, which is the gift of God.

Did Cain repent? Perhaps he did. He said that his punishment was greater than he could bear and asked God to bear it for him. Whenever one asks God to bear one's punishment for one, is not that a sign of repentance? Is it not the sinner answering God's invitation, "Cast thy burden upon the Lord"? And is not sin the heaviest and darkest of all burdens? Yes, I like to think that Cain repented and that the first murderer was saved by the grace of Christ, who Himself was slain on the cross by His brethren.

When we get to heaven and see David and Isaiah and Elijah, and Peter and James and John, and the penitent thief, and the woman who was a sinner, perhaps we shall see Cain and Abel also. No longer will they be separated by sin and hatred and death, but united forever, these two brothers, with their arms about each other, singing together the song of the redeemed: "Unto him that loved us, and washed us from our sins in his own blood, and hath made us kings and priests unto God and his Father; to him be glory and dominion for ever and ever. Amen."

8

BRASS FOR GOLD—REHOBOAM

King Rehoboam made shields of brass (2 Chron. 12:10).

After Solomon had finished the temple, he turned his attention and his interest to other buildings. Among these was a house of justice, called also the "house of the forest of Lebanon." Here was his throne of ivory, overlaid with the finest gold and guarded by twelve massive ivory lions. On three rows of cedar columns that upheld the roof were hung three hundred shields of beaten gold. They were silent witnesses to the splendor and the power of the kingdom of Judah. When Solomon went to the temple to worship God, his bodyguard bore the golden shields before him to the strains of martial music.

But now Solomon was dead. Jeroboam, the son of Nebat, had caused Israel to sin; the kingdom was divided, and Rehoboam, the son of Solomon, ruled the southern kingdom at Jerusalem. He did that which was evil in the sight of the Lord, with the inevitable consequences. At this time of decay, Shishak, the king of Egypt, came up with a great army and took Jerusalem; this was only the first of a long series of defeats and humiliations. He stripped the temple of its sacred treasures and ravished all the holy and splendid places. His greedy eye was attracted by the three hundred shields of gold that hung upon the cedar columns in the house of the forest. These, too, he seized and carried down into Egypt to tell the story of his victory over Judah.

A braver king would have sounded the trumpet, gathered his fighting men, and tried to retrieve the lost fortunes, winning back with the sword the symbols of Judah's greatness. But Rehoboam knew an easier way. Where his father had gathered gold of Ophir, he gathered brass and made three hundred shields of brass and hung them up in the place of the lost three hundred shields of gold. When he went to the temple to call upon the God whom he had forsaken, his men-at-arms carried the shields of brass before him, and they shone in the bright sunlight as if they were of the finest gold. But the men who carried them and the people who saw them borne in the procession knew that it was all a hollow show. They knew that the shields of gold had been taken by the king of Egypt and were now adorning the temples of Isis and Osiris, and that the shields of Rehoboam, paraded with so much pomp, were only common brass. "How is the gold become dim! how is the most fine gold changed!"

"Brass for gold!" That tells the story of the decline of Judah. It tells the story, too, of what often happens in the kingdom of a person's life. One day the walls of the palace of the soul, like this house in the wood, are hung with bright shields beaten out of the pure gold of honorable ambition and lofty principle. Then comes the struggle of life, the invasion of sordid motives, the temptations to ease and self-indulgence, "The hardening of the heart that brings Irreverence for the dreams of youth."

Sometimes the house is stripped of its golden shields and nothing is put in their place. But more frequently it happens in life as it happened in this trophy hall of ancient Judah: the walls are still decorated with shields, but they are brass shields that have been substituted for the gold. The individual has become content with second or third bests in achievement and character. The fine gold has gone, and in its place hangs the cheaper and ignoble brass. The brass shields hanging in Judah's famous palace were silent, yet their silence was sadly eloquent of the nation's decline. And could we pass through that hall not made with hands, the human soul, we should find there the same sad witness to the decline of that kingdom's power and beauty. This is what I should like to do for you now—

conduct you into the chamber of the soul and let you survey its walls, to see what is happening to your fine purposes, your high resolutions, and your early consecration.

WE ALL HANG SHIELDS OF GOLD

We have all fashioned shields of gold and hung them upon our walls. Take someone whose life seems abandoned to evil and whose whole existence is to do wrong and to sin against his or her own soul. You might not expect to find in that person's past any trace of fine ambitions or nobler aims. Yet that is what you will find there, if you grope long enough amid the dismal rubbish of his or her life. As in some old ruin you will come upon the fragments of a delicately traced capital or massive archway that proclaim the original beauty and splendor of what is now but a heap of rubbish, so in the life of the worst sinner or criminal, given now to sin and bestiality, you may discover the relics of a different person. Perhaps this individual once entertained hopes just as radiant as your own, set before himself or herself aims just as high as your own, hung high the golden shields of a pure and honest life and promised to reverence them to the end.

How true to life is that picture that Charles Dickens, in *The Tale of Two Cities*, paints of Sydney Carton, the gifted solicitor who had ruined his life through sin and folly. After his all night's work on the case for the court, for which he himself would receive no recognition and little remuneration, Carton left the office and started back to his miserable lodgings. The air was cold and the river dark and dim. Wasted forces within him, the man paused at the entrance to his home and saw for a moment, lying in the wilderness before him, a mirage of honorable ambition, self-denial, and perseverance.

> In the fair city of this vision, there were airy galleries from which the loves and graces looked upon him, gardens in which the fruits of life hung ripening, waters of Hope that sparked in his sight. A moment, and it was gone. Climbing to a high chamber in a well of houses, he threw himself down in his clothes on a neglected bed, and its pillow was wet with wasted tears.

As some most pure and noble face,
Seen in the thronged and hurrying street,
Sheds o'er the world a sudden grace,
A flying odor sweet;
Then, passing, leaves the cheated sense
Baulked with a phantom excellence:
So, on our soul the visions rise
Of that fair life we never led:
They flash a splendor past our eyes,
We start, and they are fled:
They pass and leave us with blank gaze,
Resigned to our ignoble days.[1]

Yes, we have all hung up our shields of gold. But alas, too often the enemy of our souls has taken them away.

Do you recall the flood of emotion that came over you that day when you were reading the book that told of some noble, unselfish life, and you said with yourself, "I will be like that man or that woman"? And you, do you not remember that morning when you finished your course at college and looked with clear eye into the uncertain future and quietly resolved that you would be faithful, if not famous? And you, do you think now of the day that love began to burn within your heart, and to its holy, cleansing, and consuming flame you consigned all that was ugly dross in your life?

And you, do you recall the day when you lay close to the grave, the candle of your life flickering faintly, and you knew not whether the wind of death would blow it out completely? Yet as you lay there with closed eyes and speechless lips and communed with your own heart, you said with yourself that if God spared your life and raised you up, henceforth you would give Him the best?

And you, have you forgotten the day when your sin and folly began to pay wages and, stricken in conscience, shaken in your soul, in the most solemn manner you repented of your sin and said, God helping you—and you knew He would help

---

1. "The Fugitive Ideal," from *The Poems of Sir William Watson, 1878–1935.* Used by permission of George G. Harrap & Co.

you—you would live henceforth a godly, righteous, and sober life?

And you, have you forgotten the hour when the Word of God as read or as preached in the church reached your heart, definitely, clearly; and there rose before you in all His incomparable majesty and pathos Jesus of Nazareth, crucified for your sins, and you said within your heart that you would follow Him and believe in Him and belong to Him for time and eternity?

No, I am sure that you have not forgotten these days. How could you forget them? You are just like any other man or woman—there was a day when you too hung up the shields of gold.

HOW SHIELDS OF GOLD ARE LOST

How fares it with your shield? In some lives one dark transgression in a single night has swept all the walls clear, leaving only bleak desolation and ruin. But in most lives the theft of the golden shields has been done quietly, stealthily, and the base substitutes hung up so noiselessly that the inmate of the palace hardly knows they are gone.

What are the reasons that this deterioration, this moral shrinkage, this substitution of the baser for the best, takes place in so many lives? One reason is that we must pay a price. Gold shields are not kept without a struggle. There are others who covet them. There are sacrifices that must be made. The moment in life when you set before you anything high and honorable, that moment you are beset by a thousand foes. Jesus called Peter to be His disciple; what a disciple Peter resolved to be, faithful, he, where all others might fail. "Although all shall be offended, yet will not I." "Lord, I am ready to go with thee, both into prison, and to death." Yes, it was for that very reason, because of his high ideal of what a disciple of Jesus ought to be, that Peter was the special object of Satan's assault. "Simon, Simon, behold, Satan hath desired to have you, that he may sift you as wheat."

Another reason that shields of gold are lost is the love of this world. One day at Rome there was a young man who happened to hear Paul preach to a group of soldiers and other attendants of the Mamertine, the prison. Paul was talking about a man Jesus who had been crucified in Jerusalem. The young man drew nearer and listened intently. There was something about this old prisoner that touched him and something about that Lord Jesus to whom he referred that moved him. The young man heard him again the next day, and the next. At length he became Paul's disciple and companion and, what is more important, the disciple of Jesus. His name is coupled with that of honored Luke and Aristarchus and Mark when Paul sends greetings to the Christians at Colosse and to Philemon. He made a fine beginning, but the ending was sad. Paul has no bitterness in his voice when he tells of the young man's fate, for he loved him. This is what he said of him: "Demas hath forsaken me, having loved this present world."

There is little danger now, as when Demas became a Christian, of being cast into prison, or burned, or thrown to wild beasts due to one's faith. Yet that sentence of Paul still stands. Wherever people prove traitors to their best selves, wherever Christian disciples forsake Jesus as that young man forsook Paul, the reason is the same—the love of this present world. O world! O world! what a deceiver you are! How quickly you can shrink and fade for us into mere nothingness! In how brief a moment, by one single blow on the head, or a fever in the blood, or a tumult in the heart, we are through with you forever, and your vain show is over! Yet how you do seduce us with your flattery and charm us with your painted face, so that in our blind infatuation and flaming love for you, for one little moment more of your unreal, corruptive joys, we sell our souls, forget our God, crucify our Lord afresh, and forego our hope of eternal happiness!

The Danish theologian and philosopher Kierkegaard has a parable of a wild goose. With his mates this goose was flying in the springtime northward across Europe. On the flight he happened to come down in a barnyard in Denmark where there were tame geese. He ate and enjoyed some of their corn and stayed—first for an hour, and then for a day, and then for a week, and then for a month, and finally, because he liked the good fare and the safety of the barnyard, stayed all summer. But one autumn day when his wild mates were winging their way southward again they passed over the barnyard, and the goose heard their cries. It stirred him with a strange thrill of joy and delight; and, flapping his wings, he rose in the air to join his old comrades in their flight to the land of summer.

But, alas, he found that his good fare had made him so soft and heavy that he could rise no higher than the eaves of the barn. So he sank back again to the barnyard and said to himself, "Oh, well, my life is safe here and the fare is good." Every spring, and again every autumn, when the wild geese flew over his barnyard and he heard their honking cry, his eye gleamed for a moment and he began to lift his wings and would fain have joined his mates. But at length the day came when the wild geese flew over him and uttered their cry and he paid not the slightest attention to them.

What a parable that is of how the soul can forget its high ideals and standards and be content with lower things!

HOW TO WIN BACK THE SHIELDS OF GOLD

What can we do when we realize that there is brass in our lives where there ought to be gold? How can we win back our lost shields? That will be harder to do than it was to lose them. Yet with God's help it is possible. The first step is to be honest in taking stock of ourselves, to confess with ourselves that here, in this or that quarter of life, have been unfaithfulness and sin. This was the first step that the lost son took in the great tale of our Lord. He "came to *himself*." He saw the contrast between that hungry, diseased, filthy herder of swine and the younger son of that far-distant home. The trouble with so many people is that they fear to face themselves. They stay away from church, from prayer, from the Bible, from sermons, from meditation—as far as possible from anything that will bring them face-to-face with themselves. They know that they have lost, and they know that they are losing now; yet they will not confess it and act upon that knowledge.

With the acknowledgment of loss there must go the determination to seek again what we have lost and to set before ourselves the same high aims that once were ours. The temptation is strong for one to accept one's present self as the finished self, the finality for this life, and to regard oneself, for better or for worse, as past change or amendment. The loss of valuable time, the memory of yesterday's failures, the intimate knowledge of the trials and difficulties that go with seeking after the best—all these rise up to discourage one from starting up the long steep hill again and returning to the Father's house. But that purpose and that effort must be there if the soul is to get back what it has lost.

The way back to God must be retraced step by step. It is not done in a day or an hour. Step by step you lost that way, and now step by step you must retrace it. In the love of human praise, in the indulgence of your desires for the things of this world, in your devotion to time and sense, in your forgetting of God until He became but a dream, and your careless, godless life became the reality—in all these ways and by these steps you left and lost the way of life. Slowly, therefore, and painfully you must find your way again. The great thing is to determine to do that, and take the first step. Let that step be taken, deny yourself some self-indulgence, lay aside some one besetting sin, make but one honest effort to live in harmony with the will of God, to live for eternity and not for time, for the world to come and not this present world. Pray as blinded Samson did at Dagon's temple: "Remember me, I pray thee, . . . only this once." Then God, who wills not that any should perish, will add to your strength day by day; increasing light from the fountain of light will stream down upon your path. Return to the Lord, and He will meet you upon your path. "Return unto the Lord, and he will have mercy . . . and to our God, for he will abundantly pardon."

9

PAUL'S DOCTOR—LUKE

Luke, the beloved physician (Col. 4:14).

Robert Louis Stevenson, who saw much of physicians in his day of sickness, dedicated his book of verse *Underwoods* to the doctors who had ministered to him and helped to relieve his suffering. In that tribute he says:

> There are men and classes of men that stand above the common herd: the soldier, the sailor, and the shepherd not unfrequently; . . . the physician almost as a rule. He is the flower . . . of our civilization; and when that stage of man is done with, only remembered to be marveled at in history, he will be thought to have shared as little as any in the defects of the period, and most notably exhibited the virtues of the race.

That was a fine tribute to the doctors. A great many fine things have been said about them, but nothing better than a short sentence from the last letter of Paul. He was in Rome and in prison, after the second trial, and was under sentence of death. In a short time he expected to be "offered up" as another victim to the wickedness of Nero. But his affectionate heart longed for companionship. Apparently, most of his Roman friends had deserted him in his hour of need, for it was now dangerous to be known as the friend of Paul. Paul writes his last letter to his dearest friend and convert Timothy, at Ephesus. He urges him to come to him, and to "come before winter," and bring with him Paul's cloak, his books, and his writing tablets. That Timothy may know Paul's present situation, he tells him: "Demas hath forsaken me, having loved this present world, and is departed unto Thessalonica; Crescens to Galatia; Titus unto Dalmatia. Only Luke is with me."

Only Luke! Time and adversity and persecution had sifted Paul's friends down to a faithful few, and among the most faithful and loyal was Luke. "Only Luke is with me." No long paragraph of eulogy, no white marble monument with lettered praise could mean half so much as that short, heartfelt tribute from the pen of the great soldier of Christ.

Luke was not only a doctor, but an author of distinction. He was the author of two of the books of the Bible, the third gospel, sometimes spoken of as the most beautiful book ever written, and the Acts of the Apostles. In this respect, Luke was the forerunner of a great company of physicians who were also men and women of letters. In this roll of honor are Servetus, who in his *Restitution of the Christian Religion* announced the discovery of the circulation of blood a hundred years before Harvey; Sir Thomas Browne, keen of observation and devout in faith—the author of the *Religio Medici*, the Religion a Doctor—who never went to call on a patient without prayer for his or her soul; among others, the poets, George Crabbe, Oliver Goldsmith, and John Keats, who left medicine for letters; Dr. John Brown of Edinburgh, who was the author of the greatest dog story ever written, *Rab and His Friends*; and in America, Oliver Wendell Holmes and S. Weir Mitchell.

Luke is seldom mentioned by name in the New Testament, but certain passages in the book of Acts, the so-called we sections, let us know when he is in the company of the apostle Paul. From this we gather that Luke was possibly a native of Antioch of Pisidia; that he joined Paul at Troas on the second missionary journey and went with him as far as Philippi; that he joined him again on the third journey at Philippi, returned with him to Jerusalem, sailed with him to Rome, and remained with him to the end of his life.

The apostle Paul, in his letter to the Galatians, refers to a sickness that overtook him when he preached in that part of Asia Minor. He also mentions a "thorn in the flesh," over the meaning of which physicians, ministers, and commentators have spilled a vast amount of ink. The fact that Luke joined Paul at Troas, as he was about to embark for Europe, suggests that Paul took Luke along, not only as a companion, but as a physician who could minister to his necessities. We like to think, therefore, that Luke, when he became a Christian, dedicated not only his personality and his literary ability to the cause of Christ, but his skill as a physician. In this respect, he was a forerunner of that long line of doctors who have served both humanity and the church of the Lord Jesus Christ.

In your imagination you can picture the two men traveling over the dusty highways of Asia Minor, or crossing the Aegean or the Mediterranean Sea, going up to Jerusalem and Ephesus, and at length to Rome. When the dangers and fatigue of the day are over, Luke gets out his medicine case and ministers to the necessities of Paul. Frequently sick, always pierced with his thorn in the flesh, Paul was yet able to endure hardships and to travel those thousands of miles by land and by sea. Perhaps Luke, under the hand of God, had much to do with the physical endurance that made possible the grand exploits of Paul.

Doctors are referred to, in the general sense, we may say, just twice in the Bible. In 2 Chronicles 16:12, it is written that "Asa in the thirty and ninth year of his reign was diseased in his feet, until his disease was exceeding great: yet in his disease he sought not to the Lord, but to the physicians. And Asa slept with his fathers." Whether the chronicler was conscious of the sequence of his thought there, we do not know. The New Testament reference is in connection with the woman who had an issue, and who had "suffered many things of many physicians, . . . and was nothing bettered, but rather . . . worse." When the doctors wish to have sport with themselves, they can use those two passages. But our tribute will be one of sincere honor and gratitude.

An old-fashioned country physician in the mountain area of Maryland, just south of the Pennsylvania line, was on his way through the woods on a dark night to make a call at one of the mountain homes, when masked bandits suddenly confronted him and ordered him to throw up his hands. As he made some exclamation, the robbers, recognizing his voice, said, "Oh, we didn't know it was you, Dr. Skilling!" With an apology they permitted him to pass. It was a fine tribute from lawless men to the service of a good physician.

The physician, more than the minister or the lawyer or the teacher, has the satisfaction of seeing quick, and sometimes immediate, results from his or her ministry. One of the pioneer doctors of western Pennsylvania was Dr. Marchand, who practiced at Sewickley Creek, about six miles west of Greensburg, as early as 1770. His hospital, built near the close of the Revolutionary War, was the first stone building in western Pennsylvania. It was designed also for a fort, and near the hospital stood his large log house, the front room of which was used as a schoolroom and as a church. The historian says of him in a naive note, "He was buried in Brush Creek Churchyard, to which he was a liberal contributor." But, as a class, the physicians have done more than any other to keep people out of the cemetery until their time has come, when no doctor, no surgery, and no potent drug can stay the hand of death.

The doctor's chief reward is the satisfaction in knowing he or she has relieved pain, spared life, and blessed human relationships. When John Watson, or Ian Maclaren, was last in this country, the physicians of Boston called on him at his hotel and presented him with a bouquet of roses as a "token of our high appreciation of your beautiful tribute to our profession in A Doctor of the Old School." When that doctor of the old school, William McLure, had saved the life of Saunders and, riding home past the kirk on the Sabbath, was cheered by the village folk and the minister himself, the doctor, talking to himself and to his horse, said: "Yon was our reward. Not many men in this world will ever get a better, for it came from the heart of honest folk."

You may have seen in a doctor's office that fine painting by L. Fields, *The Doctor*, the original of which hangs in the Tait Gallery in London. The doctor, an earnest, thoughtful, bearded man, sits by the pallet of the little sufferer in the cottage room, his head resting on his hand, his eyes observing his patient. The shaded lamp burns on the stand on which are the spoons and the glasses, filled with the medicines, ready for use. In another part of the room the mother has fallen forward on the table with her face buried in her arms, the sword of anguish and anxiety piercing her soul. At her side stands the peasant husband, his great hand resting lightly on the shoulder of his sobbing companion, and his face turned in anxious expectation toward the doctor. That picture shows a doctor at his best, as the friend of the meek and lowly, giving his time and his strength and his wisdom to save the poor man's child.

Science is the greatest influence of our day; since the doctor is the servant of science, vast is his or her influence. The kingdom is the human body—and what an empire that is! provided the doctor, in dealing with bone and artery and cell and tissue, retains the grand Christian thought of the body as the temple of God. In my congregation in Philadelphia there was an aged physician who had acted as a prosector for one of the noted surgeons of that city. He told me that when preparing the bodies for the demonstration in the dissecting room, he always tried to remember that they had once been the temple of God, the tabernacle of a human spirit, and therefore worthy of reverence.

No one knows so well the terrible record of alcohol as the doctor and is able to preach to people the most powerful and eloquent sermon on that subject. Dr. Frederick Peterson, the eminent nerve specialist of New York, had printed on every prescription blank that went from his office the following statements about alcohol:

> Alcohol is a poison. It is claimed by some that alcohol is a food. If so, it is a poisoned food. The daily regular use of alcohol, even in moderation, leads to chronic alcoholism. One is poisoned less rapidly by the use of beer than by drinking wines, gin, whiskey, and brandy. Alcohol is one of the most common causes of insanity, epilepsy, paralysis, diseases of the liver and stomach, dropsy, and tuberculosis. A father or mother who drinks poisons the children born to them. Some die in infancy, while others grow up as epileptics and paralytics.

I suppose that there are few doctors who would question any one of those statements. In this day when advertisements, public journals, and public officials are actually advocating the consumption of liquor as a desirable thing, and when there seems to be a move on to turn the United States into a vast beer garden, what a grand thing it would be if every physician had courage to talk as the doctor just quoted did about the effects of alcohol, whether consumed under prohibition, state license, or federal control! Oliver Wendell Holmes, of happy memory, told the truth about alcohol when he described it as the liquid which "destroys men's viscera when they are alive and confers immortality on those parts when they are dead."

What is true of the ravages of alcohol is true of the breaking of natural laws and of the divine laws with regard to sex; here, too, the doctor is best qualified to reiterate the divine enactments and to warn of the terrible revenge of nature.

The presence and the testimony of a physician in one's church counts for a great deal. Many today in the name of science pretend to repudiate the great truths of Christianity; whereas, science, as such, has nothing whatever to say about those great truths. The renowned doctor Sir William Osler concluded his lecture on "Science and Immortality" at Harvard University thus:

> Whether across death's threshold we step from life to life, or whether we go from whence we shall not return, even to the land of darkness, as darkness itself, the scientist cannot tell; nor is this strange. Science is organized knowledge, and knowledge is of the things we see. Now the things that are seen are temporal; of the things that are unseen, science knows nothing, and has at present no means of knowing anything.

The picture of Paul and Luke traveling together through Asia and through Europe and across the seas is a fine illustration of the relationship that ought to exist between the minister and the physician. The physician ought to be the right hand of the minister, and they together (Paul and Luke, beloved apostle and beloved physician) represent the whole area of the person's life: the body and the soul. There are times when one needs more the physician than the divine; there are also times when one needs the "divine more than the physician," and when the greatest thing that the doctor can say is to reiterate what the minister says.

In one of his stories, Dr. S. Weir Mitchell describes the

passing of a patient. When the man was gone and his heart had ceased to beat, the nurse, laying her hand on the still heart, said, "The engine has stopped." "No," said the doctor, "the engineer has departed."

Christ is the Great Physician for doctors as well as for all others. When that doctor of the old school, William McLure, was dying, he asked his friend Drumseugh to read a bit from the Bible. The laird opened to the fourteenth chapter of John's gospel and commenced at the familiar words, "In my Father's house are many mansions." But the dying doctor stopped him saying, "It's a bonnie word, but it's nae for the like of me." Then the laird let the Bible open of its own accord at the place where the doctor had been reading every night for the past week. It was the passage in which Jesus tells us what God thinks of a penitent sinner: "And the publican, standing afar off, would not lift up so much as his eyes unto heaven, but smote upon his breast, saying, God be merciful to me a sinner."

Yes, that is our message for doctors, ministers, lawyers, bankers, soldiers, and sailors—for all the people who, when they come to the end of their lives, can have nothing to say for themselves but that: "God be merciful to me a sinner." A medical student in Edinburgh once asked the discoverer of chloroform, Sir James Simpson, what he considered his greatest discovery. The man of science, and the man of God, answered: "The greatest discovery I ever made was when I discovered that I was a great sinner, and that Jesus Christ is a great Savior."

10

THE MAN WHO WAS SICK—TROPHIMUS

Trophimus have I left at Miletum sick (2 Tim. 4:20).

Trophimus has the distinction of having been not only a disciple and traveling companion of Paul, but also one of the last names on the lips of the apostle. Only four others are mentioned after Trophimus: Eubulus, Pudens, Linus, and Claudia—Christian believers at Rome.

But what interests us particularly in Trophimus is that he was left at Miletum sick. Of Paul's former traveling companions only Luke was now with him at Rome. Demas had forsaken him, "having loved this present world"; Crescens had gone to Galatia; Titus to Dalmatia; Tychicus, his amanuensis, he had sent on some errand to Ephesus; and Erastus had remained behind at Corinth. "But Trophimus have I left at Miletum sick."

Incidentally, this is one of the records which throws some light upon the last years and the last days of Paul. The book of Acts comes to a close with Paul a prisoner at Rome. If that were all, we might conclude that he was at that time brought to trial, found guilty of treason against Caesar, and put to death.

There are, however, a number of passages in Paul's first letter to Timothy, and other of his prison epistles, such as the letter to Philemon, that make it fairly certain that Paul was set free after his first trial and that he left Rome. Perhaps he fulfilled his desire and plan to visit Spain, mentioned in his letter to the Romans, "Whensoever I take my journey into Spain." Probably he then returned to Greece and Asia Minor, was arrested again, sent to Rome, tried, found guilty, and beheaded. That something like this was his history is suggested by this brief reference to Trophimus.

Trophimus was one of the converts of Paul at Ephesus. When Paul was driven out of Ephesus by the riot stirred up against him by the silversmiths, Trophimus had gone with him into Macedonia and Greece and afterward returned with him to Asia Minor and traveled with him up to Jerusalem. The others in the company were Sopater of Berea, Aristarchus and Secundus of Thessalonica, Gaius of Derbe, Timothy, Tychicus, and Luke. On that journey Paul's ship touched at Miletum, whither he summoned the elders of the Ephesian church and delivered to them his beautiful farewell address, never expecting to see them again. When he reached Jerusalem, some of the Asiatic Jews saw him in the company of Trophimus, whom they had known at Ephesus, and set up a false cry that Paul had defiled the temple by bringing Trophimus, a Gentile, into it.

It is clear, then, that when Paul in his last message says he left Trophimus at Miletum sick, it was not this journey to which he referred, for we find Trophimus with him at Jerusalem, and the innocent cause of the tumult raised against the apostle. The only reasonable explanation is that the visit to Miletum, when he left Trophimus behind him sick, was after the one to Jerusalem and, therefore, *after* Paul had been released from his first imprisonment.

TROPHIMUS LEFT BEHIND

But interesting as this verse is in the light it throws on Paul's last days, it is the sickness of Trophimus and the fact that Paul had to leave him behind as he went on his journey which hold our attention. Just where Paul was going when he left Miletum we are not certain. Probably he was on his way to visit Rome again, for we are told that one of his companions, Erastus, stayed behind at Corinth in Greece, which would be on the way.

I see Paul standing there on the quay at Miletum with some of his other companions, and again, as before, surrounded by friends who had come down from the church at Ephesus. Perhaps he told them that when he last bade them a farewell he had not expected to see them again in this world, but that through the goodness of God he had been set free after his first trial at Rome—"delivered," as he put it, "out of the mouth of the lion," that is, out of the hands of Nero.

Now the master of the little vessel on which Paul is to sail blows his horn as a signal for all passengers to go aboard. Paul gives a final benediction to his kneeling friends, and then he and those traveling with him—Luke, we can be sure, was one of them—go into the ship. The lines that hold her to the dock are cast off, the red sail is raised, the south wind blowing softly quickly fills it out, and the ship moves rapidly out of the harbor bound for the west, and Rome. Paul and those with him wave a last good-bye to the little group of disciples on the quay, and they to him.

But there was one of Paul's companions who had to be left behind. Yonder at the window of one of the homes near the dock, I can see his pale face. His Christian friends raise him up on his bed so that he can witness the departure of Paul. He lifts one hand in a feeble gesture of farewell and then falls back exhausted on his pallet. He had counted so much on going with Paul on that hazardous second journey to Rome. He knew full well the risks of such an expedition; he had been through many trials and journeys with Paul and wanted to take this journey above all the others. But Trophimus was sick—too sick to walk, too sick even to be carried to the ship. Paul, I am sure, came to visit him and pray with him, and expressed a hope for his recovery and that they might meet again on some journey for Christ; if not, then at God's right hand. But that was not to be. Trophimus had to remain behind at Miletum. "Trophimus I left at Miletum sick."

SICKNESS COMES TO ALL

Sickness is a universal experience. Once in everyone's life comes a fatal sickness. Perhaps Trophimus recovered sufficiently to be taken back to his home and friends in Ephesus; perhaps he died there at Miletum. But one thing we know—he had to be left behind because of his sickness. He was so eager, so nobly ambitious to go with Paul and share his hardships and dangers for the sake of Christ, but his sickness forbade him. How many have been held back from great undertakings by sickness, how many journeys given up, how many plans abandoned, how many good books never written, how many sermons never preached, how many pictures never painted, how many statues never chiseled, how many poems never indited, how many ministries of kindness forbidden, because of some thorn in the flesh: a weak eye, a weak back, a weak heart.

Traveling along the highway, the tourist will often come to a barrier, and near at hand the sign Detour. Life has many detours. After many miles and days of smooth going in fine spirits and with rapid progress, suddenly we come upon the sign Detour. There we must leave the good road for a rough and winding one. Sickness is a common detour. The goal may almost have been reached, the book almost finished, the prize almost attained. Then sickness stops the procession, and everything must wait.

SICKNESS AND PROVIDENCE

Sickness, like every other providence of God, has its uses, its blessings, although these, at the time, may seem hidden. The Bible, which is always so true to life, tells of many who were sick, when the whole head was sick and the whole heart faint: little children—for sickness is no respecter of age—such as David's child of his sin who died despite his father's plenteous tears and prayers; the little son of the Shunammite woman, restored to life by Elisha; Naaman, the Syrian satrap, who was a great man "but he was a leper"; Elisha himself, who healed others but could not heal himself; the great King Hezekiah, for whom the shadow ran back ten degrees on the dial of life and who, when he was recovered of his sickness, said, "By these things men live"; all those sick of divers diseases whom Jesus healed; Lazarus, who was sick and died and was restored to life by Jesus; Trophimus, left behind at Miletum; Epaphroditus, the messenger sent by the church at Philippi to minister to Paul in the prison at Rome, and who, Paul writes, "was sick nigh unto death: but God had mercy on him; . . . lest I should have sorrow upon sorrow"; and Paul himself, with that thorn piercing his flesh.

Sickness is a providence that gives opportunity for the display of Christian kindness and compassion. Among the benedictions pronounced by Jesus is that one that we all have opportunity to earn—"sick, and in prison, and ye visited me." Our greatest admiral was David Glasgow Farragut. Looking back over his illustrious career, Farragut said that he owed his fame and his great record as a commander in the Navy to an act of Christian kindness on the part of his parents. After serving the American cause in the Revolution, his father, a native of Minorca and a sailor and soldier of adventure, took up his residence at New Orleans. Living there at that time was the father of Commodore Porter, later hero of the War of 1812 and father of Admiral David Dixon Porter of Civil War fame. Becoming sick one day, the old man was taken into the home of Farragut's father and mother, where he was tenderly nursed until his death. When Commodore Porter learned of this kindness to his parent, he wished to show his gratitude to the Farragut family. Since the mother was now dead and the family in straits, Porter asked the senior Farragut to let him adopt David Glasgow, then only eight years of age. The father gave his consent, and the boy, at the now incredible age of nine years, was given a midshipman's warrant. Thus he commenced his illustrious career. "I mention this kind act on the part of my parents," wrote Farragut in his journal, "because it is to this circumstance that I am indebted for my present rank in the Navy of the United States."

The chief blessing of sickness, however, is not to those who wait upon the sick, but to the sick themselves. Sickness lets us know how all our strength can fail us and how in a day or even less, we can find ourselves, as Burns described himself in a sickness, "weak as a woman's tears." In 1893, although the country knew nothing of it at the time, a noted Philadelphia surgeon, on a yacht off Wood's Hole, operated on the twenty-fourth president of the United States, Grover Cleveland, for cancer of the throat. After his recovery Grover Cleveland made this testimony: "I have learned how weak the strongest man is under God's decree; and I see in a new light the necessity of doing my allotted work in the full apprehension of the coming night." Thus his sickness taught him two things: humility and, when his strength came back to him, new earnestness in the work of life. It said to him, "Work, for the night cometh." In the words of Jesus, "The night cometh, when no man can work."

SICKNESS AND THE SOUL

Sickness gives opportunity for the display of the heroic virtues of the soul. A French philosopher once said, "We are far from being acquainted with the whole of our will." The psalmist speaks of "all that is within me." That *all* within human possibility is very deep and great, but by many never explored. Sick men and women have given magnificent exhibitions of will power and determination and of faith. We think of Parkman, taking eighteen years to write his *Pioneers of France in the New World* because of the precarious state of his health; of Prescott, using a writing case for the blind when he wrote his monumental works, *History of the Conquest of Mexico* and *History of the Conquest of Peru*; of Robert Louis Stevenson, writing his engrossing tales while propped up on his pillows, the fire of lever in his veins; of General Grant, completing his *Memoirs*, his story of the Civil War, with cancer gripping him by the throat; of John Calvin, who hardly knew a well day, "solitary and feeble," as Bancroft describes him,

> toiling for humanity, till after a life of glory he bequeathed to the world a fortune in books and furniture, stocks and bonds, not exceeding $200, and to the world a purer Reformation, Republican liberty, and the kindred spirit of Republican institutions.

SICKNESS TEACHES PATIENCE

The bed of sickness is a school for patience. John Milton's soul burned with a high desire to write something "such as men will not willingly let die." But in his blindness he feared at first that his affliction would frustrate his great project to "assert eternal Providence and justify the ways of God to men." Yet he bore his affliction with resignation, patience, and even cheerfulness. An unknown reviler taunted him by saying that his blindness had been sent as a punishment from heaven. Answering this cruel assault, Milton wrote that noble sentence: "It is not so wretched to be blind, as not to be capable of enduring blindness." For his own comfort and for the comfort and encouragement of others who have had to pass through this valley of the shadow, he wrote the great sonnet "On His Blindness":

> When I consider how my light is spent,
> E're half my days, in this dark world and wide,
>   And that one Talent which is death to hide
> Lodg'd with me useless, though my Soul more bent
>   To serve therewith my Maker, and present
> My true account, lest He returning chide;
>   "Doth God exact day-labor, light deny'd?"
> I fondly ask; But Patience, to prevent
>   That murmur, soon replies, "God doth not need
> Either man's work or his own gifts. Who best
>   Bear his mild yoke, they serve him best, his State
> Is Kingly. Thousands at his bidding speed
>   And post o'er Land and Ocean without rest;
> They also serve who only stand and wait."

When Trophimus, sick and on his bed there by the window in Miletum, saw Paul's ship sail out of the harbor bound for Rome, his disappointment must have been great. I have no doubt, however, that his association with Paul and his Christian faith taught him, too, that "they also serve who only stand and wait."

SICKNESS AND FAITH

The two chief invalids of the Bible are Job and Paul. Both of them conquered their fears and doubts and saw the hand of God in their afflictions. Paul tells us that three times, and very earnestly, he besought the Lord to take that thorn, whatever it was, out of his flesh. His prayer was not answered; and yet, in a higher way, it was answered. His thorn was not taken from him, but Christ told him that He would give him grace sufficient to bear his trial—"for my strength is made perfect in weakness." Paul's sickness was an opportunity for Christ to show him the power of His grace. Thus Paul could say: "I take pleasure in infirmities, . . . in distresses for Christ's sake: for when I am weak, then am I strong."

When we turn to Job, the great invalid of the Old Testament, we see him emerging triumphant out of his fiery trial. In the trial of both Paul and Job, Satan is represented as "buffeting" them and endeavoring to shake their faith in God. God gave the great adversary of souls permission to try Paul and to try Job. At first, it might seem when we read that drama of Job that his faith has failed him. But not so. He was indeed perplexed and troubled, but in the end the clouds are gone, the sky is clear, and Job's faith is triumphant. He was able to say: "He knoweth the way that I take: when he hath tried me, I shall come forth as gold." Whatever the trial—sickness, sorrow, disappointment, pain—the purpose of God is always good. That is the inspired comment of James on the trial of Job: "Ye have heard of the patience of Job, and have seen the end of the Lord; that the Lord is very pitiful, and of tender mercy." When sick, or in any other trouble or trial, always remember the "end" of the Lord.

SICKNESS TO DEATH

When the messengers of Mary and Martha brought Jesus that word, "He whom thou lovest is sick," Jesus said, "This sickness is not unto death." Lazarus did indeed die and was buried. But death was not the final issue of the sickness of Lazarus, for Christ raised him from the dead, "that the Son of God might be glorified thereby." For the believer in Jesus, there is no "sickness unto death"; Jesus said, "[He that] . . . believeth in me shall never die." Uncounted multitudes who believed in Jesus have died since then. Yet for them and for us who believe in Jesus, death is not the final issue. "Though he were dead, yet shall he live again!" The resurrection of Lazarus was thus a parable and prophecy of the resurrection life for all who live in Christ.

There is only one "sickness unto death," death without hope, and that is the sickness of the soul. That sickness is sin, universal as human nature, eternal as human history. But for that sickness there is the Great Physician, who, when we repent and confess our sins, forgives them by the power of His death on the cross, reconciles us to God, and brings us at length to that home of many mansions that He has prepared for them that love Him, so that where He is, there we may be also.

In Isaiah's beautiful prophetic sketch of the holy city, the heavenly Zion, it is written: "And the inhabitant shall not say, I am sick: the people that dwell therein shall be forgiven their iniquity." No sickness! And best of all, no sin!

11

PROSPERITY OF
THE SOUL—GAIUS

Beloved, I wish above all things that thou mayest prosper
and be in health, even as thy soul prospereth (3 John 2).

Would it be safe for one who had the power to make his wish come true, to make that wish for you—that your bodily health and your worldly prosperity be brought to the level of the prosperity of your soul?

This brief third letter of John introduces us to three men in one of the early churches somewhere there in Asia Minor. One of these is a very unattractive character, the quarrelsome, loquacious, boasting Diotrephes, "who loveth to have the pre-eminence." His type still persists. The second, Demetrius, is a far different kind of man. For him there is a threefold witness to his Christian character and life: the report of all men, the opinion of John himself, and still more, of the Truth itself. His life adorned the Gospel that he professed. But it is not to either of these two men that this brief fourteen-verse letter of John is addressed; it is directed to the well-beloved Gaius. It is *to* him and *for* him that John expresses his wish, or better his prayer; for what John said was not "I wish," but, "I pray that . . . thou mayest prosper and be in health, even as thy soul prospereth."

There is much light shed in this letter on the character of

Gaius, but nothing is told us about his work or his station in life. From the record of his hospitality and charity, it may be reasonable to infer that he was a man of considerable standing. He may have been a merchant at Laodicea, or a purple seller at Thyatira, or a manufacturer at Smyrna, perhaps a scholar or teacher. But John tells us nothing as to that. What John does tell us is that whatever his occupation in life and whatever his worldly possessions or bodily health may have been, Gaius was prosperous in his soul.

Thus John proclaims what Christ proclaims and what all the Bible proclaims, the preeminence of the soul. Concerning man alone it was spoken, "[He] became a living soul."

For some reason, the word *soul*, and with it some of its sacred and immense significance, has dropped out of preaching. We hear of life and of character and of personality, but rarely do we hear of the greatest thing in a person—the soul. The soul is what Gaius was; it is what David was; it is what Judas was; it is what John was; it is what you are. The soul is man's eternal part.

No matter what test you subject it to, the soul stands preeminent. If you test it by the purpose of life, the soul comes first. What is the end and purpose of life? If it is for knowledge and wisdom, then how little one knows! If it is for fame and power, then how quickly one is forgotten! If it is for pleasure, then life is just a joke! But if the purpose of life is the trial and training of a soul, the development of moral and spiritual qualities in this life, and their coronation and reward in the life to come, then life is not an illusion, not a shadow that passes, but "Life is real! Life is earnest!"

Again, you may test the soul by endurance. It stands to reason that that comes first, and is most important, that endures longer than anything else. It is the soul that outlives all else. Everything else that we see or touch or handle has upon it the indubitable mark of temporality and transiency. But the soul cannot be measured by time. It takes the "measuring rod of the angel," the measuring rod of eternity, to measure this city of the soul.

A thousand empires rise
A thousand empires fall.
But still the eternal stars
Shine over all.

At last the shining stars
Into the night are thrust,
And suns and systems pale
Go down in dust.

But were the universe
Back into darkness roll,
Two lights death cannot dim—
God and the soul.[1]

Then, there is a third test which shows the preeminence of the soul, and that is what has been done for the soul. Jesus *said* great things about the soul, such as, "What is a man profited, if he shall gain the whole world, and lose his own soul?" But He also *did* great things for the soul. He gave Himself up to death, cruel and shameful, upon the cross for the redemption of the soul. It is that fact that Christ died for your soul that declares, above all peradventure or question or dispute, that your soul is the preeminent thing about you. Hence it is that the state of the soul, the poverty or the prosperity of the soul, is the thing of chief importance. John's salutation to Gaius, "even as thy soul prospereth," swings open a wide gate of thought and inquiry. There is no doubt about the prosperity of the soul of Gaius. What is prosperity of the soul?

GAIUS A GODLY MAN

Gaius was a good man. His soul was prospering because he was a godly man and did that which was right in the sight of the Lord. When John prayed that the business of Gaius might prosper, and that his health might be prosperous, even as his soul was, there may be a suggestion that his health at that time

---

1. Author unknown.

was not good, or that his business, whatever it was, was not prospering. But however that may have been, John desires health and worldly prosperity for his well-beloved Gaius, even as his soul was prospering.

Uprightness of life comes first. Integrity of soul is the foundation virtue. The first psalm opens the book of Psalms with an account of a godly, upright man:

> Blessed is the man that walketh not in the counsel of the ungodly, nor standeth in the way of sinners, nor sitteth in the seat of the scornful. But his delight is in the law of the Lord; and in his law doth he meditate day and night. And he shall be like a tree planted by the rivers of water, that bringeth forth his fruit in his season; his leaf also shall not wither; and whatsoever he doeth shall prosper.

That is the majestic chord which echoes through all the psalms. At the head of the holy procession of humankind walks first, and always, the good man, the good woman. When the good man lifts up his voice, all other voices—wit, beauty, fame, wealth, power—are silent because they recognize their master. "What doth the Lord require of thee, but to do justly, and to love mercy, and to walk humbly with thy God?"

The important thing is what is within the soul, not the external coverings of life. Once in Russia, in what was then St. Petersburg, I observed that wherever a building or construction was under way, what was going on within was screened and hidden from the public by a vast scaffolding and barrier of timber. The eye of the passerby saw only those gigantic wooden walls. But the real building, whether private dwelling or palace or bank or hotel, was going up within those wooden walls. So we have this outer life that we display to the world. But within is the real life, the life of the soul. What we are building there is the all-important thing.

GAIUS DID GOOD TO OTHERS

Another kind of prosperity of soul is doing good to others, blessing other lives. We know this was true about Gaius. John says that his goodness and kindness to others was so marked that he himself had frequently spoken of it to the different churches. Gaius fulfilled the blessing that was bestowed upon Abraham when God said to him, "Thou shalt be a blessing." To those who were his friends and brethren in the church and in the town where he lived and also to the stranger, Gaius showed kindness. No one can have prosperity of soul for oneself. Are you trying to live so that your life will bless others? You are rich according as you enrich others.

Reading recently once more through some of Charles Dickens' famous tales, I have been struck particularly with the female characters that he sketches. Some of them, of course, are frivolous and unworthy, but most of them are characters of rare beauty—beautiful flowers that, like the lily in the marsh, grew and flourished in a most unpromising and evil environment.

One of these is Lizzie, the noble daughter of the riverman, Gaffer, who made his living combing the Thames for driftwood and wreckage, and even corpses. A noble daughter she was to that strange father, and a noble sister also to the brother. Whatever life she touched was blessed and enriched. And the poor girl, Nancy, in *Oliver Twist*, who had known nothing from childhood but the companionship of extortioners, robbers, and murderers, gives up her life in an effort to save Oliver from those plotting his destruction.

Outstanding among these women characters of Dickens who blessed other lives was Little Nell in *Old Curiosity Shop*. So innocent, so frail, so helpless, Little Nell seemed unfitted for the rough journey of this world, with its snares and delusions, its shams, its brutalities and sensualities. With undying loyalty she strives to save her grandfather from the pit of ruin toward which his mania for gambling is driving him. Everywhere she goes she creates an atmosphere of happiness and peace. Among vagrant showmen, gypsies, peddlers, gamblers, canalmen, bargemen, furnacemen, Nell passes unhurt, untainted, unscathed, content in her life of Christian love. She demonstrates not only the practicality but the blessedness of the Christian way of life.

> She was dead! Dear, patient, noble Nell was dead! Where were the
> traces of her early cares, her sufferings and her fatigues? All gone, and

still her former self lay there unaltered in this change. Yes, the old fireside had smiled upon that same sweet face. It had passed like a dream through haunts of misery and care. At the door of the poor schoolmaster on the summer evening, before the furnace fire upon the cold, wet night; at the still bedside of the dying boy, there had been the same mild, lovely look. So shall we know the angels in their majesty after death.

GAIUS WAS RICH IN FAITH

Gains was prosperous in his soul because of his godly life and his deeds of charity and kindness. But above all, he was rich in faith. John says he walked in the truth. To do that, one must walk in faith; for by the "truth" the New Testament means the truth of salvation in Christ, who said, "I am the way, the truth, and the life." There are those who tell us today that if we take Christ as an example, as a leader, teacher, and friend, no more is required, and that it makes little or no difference as to His supreme rank or whether we believe and trust in Him as the Savior. But that is not what God says. He says, "This is my beloved Son: hear him." And this is what the Bible says: "Without faith it is impossible to please [God]." "If thou shalt confess with thy mouth the Lord Jesus, and shalt believe in thine heart that God hath raised him from the dead, thou shalt be saved." Faith is the fountain source of our strength and hope. Faith is just what John called it in the first of these three letters of his, "the victory that overcometh the world." Gaius was winning that victory, and he was winning it through faith in the Son of God. Faith claims two worlds for her own, this present world of battle and trial and probation, and the world that is to come:

> Far into distant worlds she pries,
> And brings eternal glories near.

Such, then, are the riches and the prosperity of the soul. Tested by these standards, how prosperous is your soul? Jesus told us of a man who was prosperous in goods and, up to the end, in health of body; but he was not rich toward God. Just when he was planning to extend his business interests and build larger barns and storehouses and was saying to his soul, "Thou hast much goods laid up for many years; . . . eat, drink, and be merry," the death sentence fell. God said to him: "This night thy soul shall be required of thee: then whose shall those things be . . . ?" Those barns, those storehouses, those fields, those cattle and sheep? "So is he that . . . is not rich toward God." David Garrick once took his old friend and tutor Samuel Johnson out to view his home at Hampton Court. He showed him the gardens, the flowers, the trees, the fountains, the tapestries, the chambers, the hallways, and the paintings, and waited for a comment from his friend. What Johnson said was this: "These are the things that make a deathbed terrible."

A few years ago everyone was reading the front-page story in the newspapers about the search for an aged recluse who had lived with his brother in one of the brownstone mansions of upper Fifth Avenue, New York. When the police finally entered the house in search of this man, they found it crowded from cellar to attic with a strange assortment of furniture, goods, papers, magazines, cables, automobile parts—almost everything that one could name. A great crowd assembled as these different articles were thrown out of the house onto the street by the police in their search for the missing man. Through the vast heaps of papers, magazines, and household goods, the man had dug tunnels from one chamber to another and, in fear of burglars, had set booby traps. At length, they found the dead man where he had been buried by a landslide of these things that he had piled up through many years. The man was choked and killed by the "things" that he had gathered and hoarded. That is a parable of what happens to not a few souls. "Whose shall those *things* be? . . . So is he that layeth up treasure for himself, and is not rich toward God."

One of the aids to prosperity of soul is doing what I trust many of you are doing now, not just reading a sermon, but thinking about the welfare of your soul. Self-examination is one of the chief safeguards of the soul. The injury, defilement, or loss of a soul through sin is always a tragedy; it has an added element of pathos and sadness when we reflect how souls are often allured to their ruin because of inattention and for the lack of self-examination. One who has traveled much in tiger-infested countries and is supposed to speak with authority has written that no man who sees the tiger before the animal sees him is ever killed by it, the reason being that the tiger always attacks from the rear. His attack must always be a surprise. If the man has seen the tiger first, it will not attack him. However that may be in the animal kingdom, it is undoubtedly true in the moral and spiritual world. Temptations that have been seen in advance, and prayed against, and guarded against, and thus fought against in advance, have little power to hurt the soul.

With self-examination goes prayer. No garden will bear fruit or flowers unless it be watered, and no soul will know prosperity unless it be watered with prayer.

What about you tonight? Would it be safe for one who has the power to make the wish come true, to wish and pray for you that your worldly affairs and your health might prosper according to the prosperity of your soul? Christ finished the Sermon on the Mount with the story of two houses. Suppose, now, I finish this sermon on the soul with the story of two houses.

Here is one house, and what a fine and noble mansion it is! But look! A change is coming over it. The roof has fallen in; the walls of stone, or brick, or marble, have changed to shabby boards; the noble entrance has become a narrow doorway; the spacious yard has shrunk to mean dimensions; the bright lights have been extinguished; the paintings on the walls have fallen to the floor; the costly Oriental rugs have been reduced to wretched rags. What was a mansion and a palace a short time ago is now just a hovel. Why? Because the earthly prosperity of the man and his physical well-being have been reduced to the level of the prosperity of his soul.

But here is another change—and a different one. In this low, humble cottage lives a godly soul. But look! The roof has been lifted up until it assumes a lofty position. The unpainted boards of the walls have been transformed into stone or marble; the mean entrance has become a noble archway; the shabby pathway and yard have expanded into a stately driveway and a beautiful lawn. The once bare floors are covered with rugs; the flickering, smoking lamps have suddenly changed into costly candelabra hung with silver cords. What is the secret of this change, this mysterious transformation? The secret of it is this: the man's temporal prosperity, his earthly habitation, his bodily health, have been brought up to the level of the prosperity of his soul.

"Even as thy soul prospereth!" How fares it with your soul? Is it safe for me to wish for you what John wished for his friend Gaius, that "thou mayest prosper and be in health, even as thy soul prospereth"?

12

THE MAN WHO CAME BACK—LAZARUS

Lazarus, come forth (John 11:43).

And Lazarus came forth, for the voice that echoed that day in the gloomy cavern of death at Bethany was the voice of Him who said: "I am he that liveth, and was dead; and, behold, I am alive for evermore . . . and have the keys of hell and of death."

Jesus once said that the foxes had holes and the birds of the air had nests, but the Son of Man had not where to lay His head. There was one home, however, where He was always a beloved and welcome guest, that home in Bethany where Lazarus lived with his two sisters, Mary and Martha. Bethany is a little village two miles from Jerusalem on the southeastern slope of the Mount of Olives, just where the road pitches steeply down the hill to Jericho.

One evening, on returning home from superintending work in his vineyards or from business in Jerusalem, Lazarus was feeling unwell. His solicitous sisters put him to bed and gave him such homely medicines as they knew, but in the morning he was no better. Then they probably called in the local leech, or physician, who left his prescriptions. The next morning Lazarus was no better, but rather worse. The anxious sisters exchanged glances and each saw mirrored in the other's face

103

the same thought—"Jesus. If only He were here!" Jesus was
then far off, beyond the Jordan. In the message they sent to
Jesus they did not say: "Come at once. We need you. Lazarus
is very sick"; but only this: "He whom thou lovest is sick." The
rest they would leave to Jesus. When Jesus received that message He said to the messengers, and to the disciples, "This
sickness is not unto death, but for the glory of God, that the
Son of God might be glorified thereby." How strange that
must have seemed to those who heard it then, and to the two
sisters. Then, instead of going at once to Bethany, Jesus remained where He was for two days.

Back at Bethany the two sisters were waiting and watching,
each taking her turn, one by the bedside of Lazarus, the other
at the shoulder of the hill where the road comes up from
Jericho. And every time they saw in the distance a traveler
coming up the hill, they said to themselves, "That will be He,
and those with Him are the disciples"; but every time, when
the traveler drew near they were disappointed.

Meanwhile, came death, who never tarries, never is late,
always on time. Lazarus died and was buried. A great stone
was rolled to the door of the sepulcher, and the sisters departed to their lonely home. No doubt while they reviewed the
events of the last sad days, as the bereaved are wont to do, they
thought of things they might have done that were left undone.
"I saw he was not looking well the day before he came home
sick. If only we had kept him home that day." Or, "If only we
had called the doctor sooner." But always the thought upper-
most in their minds was this—"If only Jesus had been here!"

At the end of two days, Jesus, knowing that Lazarus was
dead, either by a second messenger or by divine intuition, said
to His disciples: "Our friend Lazarus sleepeth; but I go, that I
may awake him out of sleep." And there, by itself, incidental as
it were, is a great utterance on immortality—Lazarus, although
in his grave, was still the friend of Jesus. Death cannot sever!
The disciples said, just as you and I would have said, "Lord, if
he sleep, he shall do well." How often anxious friends keeping
vigil by the bedside of the sick, when at length they saw the
sick man fall into a sleep, have said: "He is asleep. He shall do
well, and get well."

But Jesus was speaking of another sleep and told the disciples plainly: "Lazarus is dead. And I am glad for your sakes that I was not there." How strange that too must have seemed to them. He whom Jesus loved was dead, and yet He was glad!

Four days had elapsed since Lazarus died before Jesus came to Bethany. When Martha was told that He was coming, she ran to meet Him and said, "Lord, if thou hadst been here, my brother had not died." Not a rebuke, or a complaint, but only a regret that He had not been there when Lazarus became ill. Jesus said to her, "Thy brother shall rise again." Martha answered, "I know that he shall rise again in the resurrection at the last day." Then Jesus spoke His great words, too great for Martha to take in then, and almost too great for you and me today, "I am the resurrection, and the life."

Evidently Jesus had asked about Mary, for Martha hurried back to the house, still filled with mourners, and taking Mary aside, said to her, "The Master is come, and calleth for thee." When Mary heard that, she ran to the place where Jesus was, and falling at His feet she repeated the same words that Martha had spoken, "If thou hadst been here, my brother had not died." Jesus then asked, "Where have ye laid him?" They answered, "Lord, come and see." As they started for the sepulcher, and Jesus saw Mary and Martha weeping, and the sympathizing friends and neighbors weeping, Jesus Himself wept. "Jesus wept." When the Jews saw Him weeping, they said one to another: "Behold how he loved him! . . . Could not this man, which opened the eyes of the blind, have caused that even this man should not have died?"

Now they have come to the end of their short journey, that place where all life's journeys end, the sepulcher. There Jesus gave the first of three commands: "Take ye away the stone." But Martha, thinking that He wanted to look once more on the face of His friend, said: "Oh no, Lord; he has been in the grave four days." But Jesus, disregarding her expostulation, uttered His second command. Standing at the open door of the sepulcher, He cried in a loud voice, "Lazarus, come forth!" The sheeted dead in the cave of death heard that voice and obeyed it, for it was the voice of Him who said, "All that are in the graves shall hear his voice, and shall come forth." Lazarus came forth. But he was still bound, hand and foot and head, with the grave clothes. Jesus then spoke His third command, "Loose him, and let him go!" What followed, John leaves to our imagination; I leave it to yours. What a reunion that night in the Bethany home! When the sun rose that morning there was sorrow and mourning, but when the sun went down that evening it was a home of joy. The neighbors were there, the disciples were there, Mary and Martha were there, Lazarus was there, and He who brought him back was there.

The raising of Lazarus is the monarch among the miracles of Jesus. It takes more space and is related with greater detail than any other. The end for which it was wrought is clearly stated: for the comfort of broken hearts, for the confirmation of the faith of the disciples, for the glory of God and of the Son of God. Great too were the effects of it, for many of the Jews believed on Jesus because of the resurrection of Lazarus. This great work of Jesus yields, nineteen centuries after it took place, three all-important truths: first, the compassion and sympathy of Jesus; second, the marvelous workings of divine providence; and third, the believer's victory over death.

THE COMPASSION AND SYMPATHY OF JESUS

When Jesus started for the grave and saw Mary and Martha weeping, and the friends who were with them, "Jesus wept." That is the shortest verse in the Bible, but we could no more spare it than we could spare those verses that tell of the birth of Jesus, His crucifixion, His resurrection, or His ascension into heaven. As on an early summer morning, a single drop of dew, bathing the lips of a flower or a blade of grass, reflects the whole glory of the orient sun, so this shortest verse in the Bible reflects all the love and compassion of Christ.

But why, since in a few minutes He was going to call Lazarus back to life, did Jesus weep? Did He weep because, for the wise ends of God's providence, He was going to call Lazarus back to this world? One of the most remarkable instances of spiritual trance, or vision, is that recorded of the younger William Tennent, one of that distinguished family who contributed so much to the church and the kingdom in America. He was preparing for his examinations before the presbytery, when he suddenly collapsed and, apparently, was dead. But on the day set for the funeral, when the company had assembled at the house, the body showed signs of life. Restoratives were quickly applied, and after a considerable time he was restored to fullness of health.

It was only on rare occasions that Tennent would speak of his experience; when he did, he told how he found himself in a world of ineffable glory and saw hosts of happy beings. But when he asked his angel guide if he might join them, the angel gave him an answer which pierced his heart like a sword: "You must go back to earth." It was then that in his great distress he fainted and lay as dead for two days. So some have thought that Jesus wept because He was going to call Lazarus back to life's probation and trial, where he must again pass through the narrow gate of death.

But that certainly was not why Jesus wept. His tears were tears of compassion and sympathy. They reveal the fullness of His humanity, joined with His deity. It is John who lays such great stress on the deity of Jesus. His gospel commences with the statement that the Word was with God, and the Word was God, and ends with the statement that "these [things] are written, that ye might believe that Jesus is the Christ, the Son of God." Yet it is John who also tells us how Jesus sat weary and thirsty at the well of Jacob and asked the woman of Samaria for a drink, and here he tells us that Jesus wept.

Forty days after the Resurrection, Jesus was taken up into heaven. The Scriptures tell us that there He "ever liveth to make intercession for [us]." If, in some hour of distress or temptation or sorrow, it comforts you to remember that there are at least a few friends who think of you and pray for you, then what shall we say of the comfort and presence of our Eternal Friend, who has said He will never leave us or forsake us? There is no place where earth's sorrows are more keenly felt than up in heaven. In the words of that perfect line from William Blake, "He doth sit by us and moan." Christ's chosen three—Peter, James, and John—slept when He was in His agony, but He is the friend who never sleeps. Him no prison doors, no hospital wards, no exile, no persecution, can keep out; in Him we have one who is touched with a feeling for our infirmities. "In all their affliction He was afflicted, and the angel of His presence saved them: in His love and in His pity He redeemed them."

THE MARVELOUS WORKINGS OF DIVINE PROVIDENCE

Until the very end, all that Jesus said and did on this occasion seemed very strange. When He received the message that the one whom He loved was sick, He delayed for two days, during which time Lazarus died. When Jesus told the disciples that Lazarus was dead, He indicated that He was glad. And when He came to Bethany, four days after the death of Lazarus, and asked to be shown the sepulcher, Mary and Martha and the disciples must have thought that it was only to weep at the grave of His friend. But in the end all was made clear. The sickness of Lazarus was "not unto death"; that is, death was not to be the final issue of it.

All that Jesus said of this sickness and death turned out to be true. It was not, finally, to death; it was for the glory of God and for the glory of the Son of God; it confirmed the faith of the disciples; it brought great numbers to believe on Jesus—so many, indeed, that the leaders at Jerusalem called a special session of the Sanhedrin to see what they should do. It was then that Caiaphas, the high priest, told them that it was "expedient . . . that one man should die for the people." The cruel counsel of Caiaphas was adopted and the death of Jesus was voted. But Caiaphas was an unconscious prophet; for, in a sense far beyond what he meant, it was expedient that Jesus should die for the people and for you and me today. Thus you may say that it was the raising of Lazarus which nailed Jesus to the cross. Thus the mercy and the glory of God in redemption was revealed.

Wonderful indeed are the workings of Providence. Take the history of Joseph. Up to the very end, everything that happened to Joseph seemed to be sinking him deeper and deeper into the pit of misfortune and despair: the jealousy of his brothers and the plot to slay him; the failure of the plan of the less cruel brother, Reuben, to deliver him; the sale of Joseph to the Ishmaelites for twenty pieces of silver; his sale in Egypt on the slave block to the house of Potiphar; his resistance to the temptress; her cruel accusation; his being cast into the dungeon; the ingratitude of the chief butler whose dream he had interpreted—all this seemed to be pushing Joseph down into darkness.

But in the end, there is Joseph with Pharaoh's golden chain about his neck and, by his wisdom and power as prime minister, saving not only Israel from starvation and death, but the whole kingdom of Egypt. No wonder that Joseph said to his brothers when he made himself known to them: "It was not you that sent me hither, but God."

When the temple of Solomon was built, King Hiram of Tyre sent his lumbermen into the mountains where they cut down the cedar trees, dragged them down the mountainside to the sea, and floated them in rafts to the coast of Palestine, where they were taken up to Jerusalem and fitted into the temple. But anyone who visits the one remaining grove of the Cedars of Lebanon, far up the bleak mountainside, back of Tripoli, will wonder how from those trees—impressive, graceful, but strangely branching trees, with hardly a yard of straight timber in them—beams were hewn for the temple. It must have taken an immense amount of sawing, cutting, hewing, and splicing before they were laid in the temple. So one of the old fathers wrote: "The temple of God is a cedar one, but the cedars were all gnarly trees before He cut them down. All the carvings of heaven are made out of knots."

Out of the gnarls of life, faith in God carves out true Christian character. The English Book of Common Prayer gives the Psalms in an earlier translation than our King James Version. The great last verse in the Twenty-seventh Psalm, "Wait on the Lord: be of good courage, and he shall strengthen thine heart," in the Prayer Book reads, "O tarry thou the Lord's leisure." James wrote of a sorely tried man, who at length came forth as gold: "Ye have heard of the patience of Job, and have seen the end of the Lord; that the Lord is very pitiful, and of tender mercy." Yes, God's "end" is always good.

VICTORY OVER DEATH

When we say "victory over death," how great must be that victory; for death himself is such a victor, such a conqueror! From that "fell arrest" there is no exemption. After you have met all other of life's enemies, you must meet what Paul called the "last" enemy. For time, for this world, death writes "finis" to all achievements, to all ambition, and to even the most tender associations. Whether they be words of praise, or words of slander and denunciation, or the echo of the salutes of guns fired over their graves, the dead hear them not.

One of the world's most celebrated men, Sir Walter Raleigh, lying under sentence of death in the Tower of London, wrote thus of death:

> O eloquent, just, and mighty death! Whom none could advise, thou hast persuaded; what none hath dared, thou hast done; and whom all the world hath flattered, thou only hast cast out of the world and despised. Thou hast drawn together all the far-stretched greatness, all the pride, cruelty and ambition of man, and covered it all over with these two narrow words, *Hic Jacet* (Here Lieth).

Yet here we see Jesus victorious over death, and He promises victory over death to all who believe in Him. When He told Martha that her brother would rise again and Martha said, "I know that he shall rise again in the resurrection at the last day," Jesus answered: "I am the resurrection, and the life: he that believeth in me, though he were dead, yet shall he live: and whosoever liveth and believeth in me shall never die." Only one who is God Himself could be permitted such a paradox, such an apparent contradiction of the facts of life. Hear what He says: "Whosoever liveth and believeth in me shall never die." But have not thousands upon thousands died who believed in Jesus? And of all that great host of those who have died, who among them has come back to life? Who has ever returned from the borne of that "undiscovered country"?

In these words of Jesus there must therefore lie a deeper meaning than appears on the surface; not that believers are exempt from physical death, but that faith in Christ creates in the soul of the believer a principle and fact of life over which death has no dominion. And who has not felt that to be true when some trusting soul who loved the Lord and followed in His steps was taken away? There was something there that death could not touch, and you began to understand the meaning of the apostle's defiance of death, which once perhaps was mere rhetoric to you: "O death, where is thy sting? O grave, where is thy victory?"

Jesus, so far as we are told, brought only three persons back to life: the little daughter of Jairus, who had just died; the widow's son, in the town of Nain, who was being borne to the grave; and Lazarus, who had been in his grave for four days. Although there must have been hundreds of homes where a little daughter had died, the only person to whom Jesus said, *"Talitha cumi"* ("Damsel, arise"), was the ruler's daughter. There must have been many widows in the land who were following the bier of their only sons to the grave; yet the only person to whom Jesus said, "Young man, . . . arise," was the son of the widow of Nain. There must have been scores of little Bethanys in Palestine where a beloved brother had died, mourned by his sisters; but the only one at the door of whose sepulcher Jesus stood and cried, "Come forth," was Lazarus.

What does this tell us? It tells us that the miracles of Jesus are not only works of comfort and mercy, revelations of the power of God, proofs of the deity of Jesus, and deeds which brought people to believe on Him. But also descriptions, predictions, prophecies, apocalypses, as it were, of the life to come, where none shall say, "I am sick," and where there shall be no more death.

When Lazarus was brought back to life, did his sisters, or anyone else, ask him what he had seen and heard on the other side? No, or else "something sealed the lips of that evangelist." When they gave that banquet in the house of Simon in honor of Jesus, and grateful, loving Mary broke the box of costly ointment to anoint the feet of Jesus, wiping His feet with her hair, she asked Lazarus no questions. Martha was there, the disciples were there, the neighbors were there, Lazarus was there, and Jesus who brought him back was there; with that

Mary was content. So will it be with glad reunions in the life to come.

This great act of divine mercy, power, and compassion was done to a friend of Jesus, one whom He loved, and also for the other friends of Jesus. All the things said here of the Resurrection and of eternal life are spoken of the friends of Jesus. This then is the personal and practical question: Are you a friend of Jesus? Sooner or later, every home sends out that message, "He whom thou lovest is sick"; to every home, sooner or later, comes that same message. What could your sisters, your brothers, say of you? Could they say, "He whom thou lovest is sick"? Are you His friend?